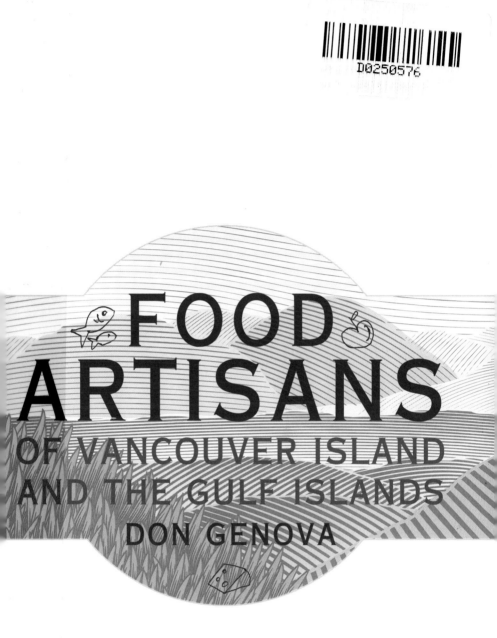

FOOD ARTISANS

OF VANCOUVER ISLAND
AND THE GULF ISLANDS
DON GENOVA

FOREWORD BY JO-ANN ROBERTS

TouchWood
Editions

TouchWood Editions
touchwoodeditions.com

LIBRARY AND ARCHIVES CANADA CATALOGUING IN PUBLICATION
Genova, Don, author
Food artisans of Vancouver Island and
the Gulf Islands / Don Genova.

Includes index.
Issued in print and electronic formats.
ISBN 978-1-77151-069-1

1. Local foods—British Columbia—Vancouver Island.
2. Local foods—British Columbia—Gulf Islands. 3. Food
industry and trade—British Columbia. I. Title.

HD9000.5.G455 2014   338.1'97112   C2013-906763-9

Editor: Marlyn Horsdal
Proofreader: Vivian Sinclair
Design: Pete Kohut
Cover image: blue67sign, istockphoto.com
Interior photos by Don Genova unless annotated.

We gratefully acknowledge the financial support for our publishing activities
from the Government of Canada through the Canada Book Fund, Canada
Council for the Arts, and the Province of British Columbia through the
British Columbia Arts Council and the Book Publishing Tax Credit.

This book was produced using FSC®-certified, acid-free paper,
processed chlorine free and printed with vegetable-based inks.

The information in this book is true and complete to the best of the author's knowledge.
All recommendations are made without guarantee on the part of the author.
The author disclaims any liability in connection with the use of this information.

1   2   3   4   5   18   17   16   15   14

PRINTED IN CANADA

To my mother and father, who laboured every day to provide our family with good food from our garden.

CONTENTS

Sunset on the west coast of Vancouver Island

VANCOUVER ISLAND REGIONS

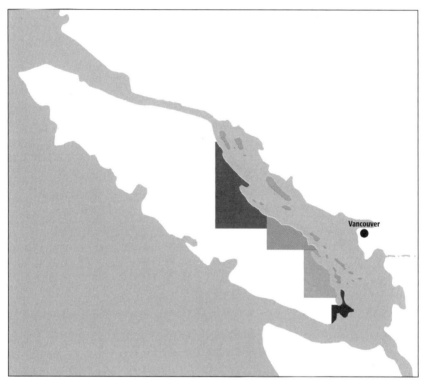

I first met Don Genova the way many people do—on the radio. I was hosting a CBC Radio morning show on the East Coast; he was a national food columnist based on the West Coast. We played his column every week on our show. He and I had never met or even talked, but like so many listeners, Don and I quickly became "radio friends." I loved his passion for everything related to food—trends, recipes, equipment, books, and people. As the mother of four school-aged children with a full-time job, my food world ran the risk of being reduced to what the kids would eat and what I could get on the table quickly. But hearing Don on the radio would inspire me to try something different or expand my family's palate.

Just before I ended up moving to the West Coast, I learned that Don was planning to visit Moncton, New Brunswick, where I was living. I was so excited for the chance to meet him. I took my tape recorder and arranged to meet Don in the kitchen of a very accomplished chef at a rather posh hotel. I had lived in the city for almost a decade and had never been invited into the hotel's kitchen to meet the chef. We not only met him, but the chef also prepared an amazing meal of local foods for Don, and me, as it turned out, to sample. I did an interview with both Don and the chef about the meal to run on the show the next day. It was the beginning of a delicious friendship.

Shortly after that working lunch in the hotel kitchen, in 2004, I found out that I would be moving to Victoria to host a new afternoon show for Vancouver Island, the Gulf Islands, and the Sunshine Coast. One of the first people to learn the news was Don. I remember teasing him: "Now when you talk about food I won't have to imagine it, I'll be able to taste it because I'm going to insist you come into the studio with samples." And he has, almost every week for the past ten years. (There have been a few exceptions, like when he was away or the year he was studying in Italy.)

With our weekly chats about island food artisans, Don has continued my food education. I have loved my role as enthusiastic student and taster. The audience loves him too. I often meet people who say, "You were really enjoying that orange coconut brioche Don brought in for you." And when Don posts a recipe on our website the number of visits spike. His column is the most downloaded audio as well.

I have tried locally made cured meats, organic sodas, Phrog gin, and Fry bread. I've tasted Denman Island chocolate and admired Cosmo knives. I even considered becoming a barista just so I could have my own Reg Barber coffee tamper. I go to Cook Culture and Capital Iron for cool gadgets and have a tea-brewing cup that Daniela Cubelic of Silk Road Tea helped design. And I never drive by Drumroaster in Cobble Hill without stopping for an Americano and sometimes a brioche. All thanks to Don.

Even more importantly I have learned to seek out farmers, chefs, and other regional food artisans, some of whom I have heard about from Don and others I have found on my own because Don has raised my awareness and heightened my senses. Knowing Don has made my world a richer, more sustainable, and delectable place. He has helped me savour Vancouver Island and the Gulf Islands. I hope that reading this book will do the same for you.

—Jo-Ann Roberts
Host, *All Points West*, CBC Radio One

INTRODUCTION

When I first came to Vancouver Island as a typical tourist, I made the same vow I'm sure many other visitors have probably made: "Someday I'm going to live here." Over the course of several more visits, that vow was reaffirmed many times, and finally, in 2003, I did make the move. I settled in the Cowichan Valley, a perfect base from which to explore many parts of the region. I have been lucky enough to see the island and the Gulf Islands from the air, from the water, by bicycle, on foot, and of course by car. It's a region best seen in as many ways as possible, especially when it comes to your palate. A walk in the woods yields juicy wild berries or earthy mushrooms; boating means great fishing, crabbing, and shrimping; and cycling on a hard-packed sand beach at low tides allows for scooping up oysters and digging for clams. I hop in my car to visit blueberry farms, hazelnut groves, and apple orchards. Then there are the growing numbers of farmers' markets, wineries, cideries, and distilleries.

Over my years of exploring, I have met some very special people. They are the food and beverage artisans I talk about on my CBC Radio segment every week and they are all people who take great pride in their work and display a passion for the products they create. Whether they are farmers growing fresh ingredients, cheese makers coaxing curds from fresh cow's, sheep's, or goat's milk, or chocolatiers crafting mouth-watering sweets, they all work very hard to make wonderful stuff for us to eat or drink.

The best part about our artisan culture is that it is growing at a rapid pace, aided by the way our coastal food culture is changing. More than ever, people care about where their food comes from and how it is produced, and they are driving the production of local cheeses, pasture-raised beef and chicken, and even sea salt from the waters around our islands. There are far more farmers' markets now than there were ten years ago. You can even find them in urban parking lots and next to office buildings.

The average age of a farmer in Canada is around fifty-two, and some artisans in the meat-processing business have retired or simply closed their businesses because of changes in meat inspection regulations. (The new regulations often required expensive modifications and upgrades to existing processing plants that the butchers simply couldn't afford.) You might think losing these experienced veterans would hamper local production, but somehow I feel a change is upon us. I've met many young people over the past few years who are either getting into farming or, more frequently, developing artisan food products. They are brave and bold and aren't necessarily taking over a family business. In fact, it's more likely they've come to a realization they don't want nine-to-five office jobs and don't mind getting into something they make and own themselves, even if it means getting dirty and working from dawn until after dark.

While I prefer to eat and drink food and beverages made from local ingredients, I have a far-ranging palate. I'm not going to give up coffee, lemons, olive oil, or cinnamon just because you can't produce those commodities on Vancouver Island. That's why in this book I tell you where to find the best olive oils or spices from faraway countries. But keep in mind that we still produce a woefully small percentage of the food we eat on these islands, so where there is a choice, please purchase locally. You'll encourage the growth of community-owned businesses and support people who really deserve your patronage.

This book is meant to salute and share my knowledge of all the great artisans and shopkeepers and farmers I've met during the twenty-plus years I've lived in British Columbia. I want to pass on their stories of how they got started, or why I like their products in particular. No snapshot in time like this book could cover all the artisans who are out there, but

I can tell you that I've visited each and every one of the businesses listed here or sampled their products. I am sharing my favourites and asking you to trust my judgment. It's not too much of a stretch; with my eating history, I have a pretty good idea of what makes an excellent product! I may not mention your personal favourite, but I would love to hear about it so more artisans can be included in a future edition of this book.

How to Use this Book

I've split the artisans featured in this book into different categories, so if you're looking for seafood, page through that section; the same for chocolate, specialty beverages, and so on. Some artisans may be mentioned in several sections as their businesses are diverse: Organic Fair in Cobble Hill, for example, manufactures chocolate, roasts coffee, and blends spice rubs as well as soda syrups. This book isn't designed as a typical travel guide, although you will have to travel to various corners of the island and Gulf Islands to find some of these products as they may be available only at farm-gate shops or particular retailers; others will be available at your local grocery store or through a few clicks to do a mail order on your computer. Many smaller shops will happily bring in a product for you if you can demonstrate your continued demand and loyalty.

But no matter where you live or where you visit, just page your way through the different sections of this book to find something good to eat or drink. If the travel bug does hit you, make sure you check the section on day trips that will leave your appetite sated and your cloth shopping bags and cooler full of enough goodies to keep you happy in the days ahead. When you get those bags and coolers home, have a look at the recipes scattered throughout the book, from me and some of my friends, that will help you use some of the products you've purchased. Check the websites or Facebook pages of the companies listed for the latest details on products, business hours, phone numbers, and addresses.

A Few Words about Sustainability

Shoppers want it all these days: local, seasonal, certified organic, and sustainable. Over the past few years, the word "sustainable" has become a catchword not only for the environmental movement but also for marketers and entrepreneurs eager to hitch a ride on the desires of those who want to be more careful with their purchasing power. But what is sustainability? The definition of sustainability that the David Suzuki Foundation has used before comes from the United Nations World Commission on Environment and Development back in 1987: Sustainability is "meeting the needs of the present generations without compromising the ability of future generations to meet their needs."

For a little more detail, look at the foundation's *Sustainability within a Generation* document: "Sustainability means living within the Earth's limits. In a sustainable future, no Canadian would think twice about going outside for a walk or drinking a glass of tap water. Food would be free from pesticide residues, antibiotics, and growth hormones. Air, water, and soil would be uncontaminated by toxic substances. In a sustainable future, it would be safe to swim in every Canadian river and lake; safe to eat fish wherever they were caught. Clean, renewable energy would be generated by harnessing the sun, the wind, water, and heat of the Earth."

That's a mouthful. But look at the clues contained within the statement "Food would be free from pesticide residues, antibiotics, and growth hormones." That's your key to seek out organic meats and produce and seafood from uncontaminated waters. What about when you see farmers advertising "no spray" or "pesticide free" produce at the farmers' markets? Well, that's not certified organic, and organic goes beyond the non-use of herbicides and pesticides. That's when your own judgment has to come into play. Talk to the farmer. Ask how the vegetables were grown. Do his or her chickens have access to the open air? What do they eat? If you do want to eat in a more sustainable fashion as per the definition above, you have to get a little homework under your belt. It's a good idea to learn the difference between free-range and free-run, what pastured poultry is and what the benefits of eating grass-fed beef or lamb can be.

No doubt you'll come across the phrase "100-mile diet." I've interviewed the writers who coined that phrase and they told me they picked the figure arbitrarily out of the air. Even though they're Canadians living with the metric system, they thought the "100-mile diet" sounded better

Cowichan Valley morel mushrooms are a springtime delight.

than the "160-kilometre" diet. The concept of looking for lower food miles (or kilometres), i.e., food that hasn't been shipped to you from great distances, is noble on the surface. The celebrated farmer/photographer/ author/activist Michael Ableman of Salt Spring Island once said at a talk I attended, "I'd rather eat a non-organic bunch of broccoli grown on a farm down the street than an organic bunch of broccoli shipped in from Chile." Local is better, right? Usually.

But is there anything wrong with eating mangoes from Mexico or drinking coffee from Panama when these products are produced by fairly paid farmers and transported in large quantities by boat instead of fuel-gobbling jets? People in Third World countries are depending on us for a living as well. You'll come across many conundrums such as this when you are trying to live a more sustainable lifestyle. Choosing sustainable sea-food is like shooting at a moving target. A species that was green-lighted by a monitoring agency this year may end up on the "exercise caution" or "endangered" list next year.

You could try eating according to "foodsheds." A foodshed can be defined as "a local bioregion that grows food for a specific population," but your personal definition may also depend on your choices regarding how and where the food is produced and how it gets to you. Because I live in Cobble Hill, I would mostly define my foodshed as the Cowichan Valley. Many of the vegetables, meats, and dairy products I consume are grown and produced within the valley. But my foodshed expands to include states like California and Florida, for some of my tropical fruits, and Mexico or other coffee-producing countries, because I choose to consume foods from those countries. So I choose first to purchase foods in my immediate foodshed, then try to be careful about what I purchase from other supply lines. I want my coffee to be fair trade or direct trade; the same for my bananas, and so on. But you know what? I have bought some very tasty kiwi fruit that was grown in Central Saanich. Look around for what you want. At the end of it all, no one can tell you exactly what the "right" choices are when it comes to the food you buy. It's up to you. Here are some of the definitions you'll come across on labels and signs while you are shopping for food.

Certified Organic, Transitional Organic, Organic: Certified organic foods must be grown without the use of synthetic fertilizers and pesticides and are not genetically modified organisms. They are processed without the addition of artificial flavours and colours. All the ingredients and other processes that go into making a certified organic product must be certified organic as well. For example, a certified organic chicken must be fed certified organic chicken feed and that feed must be produced with certified organic ingredients. A product that has been certified organic means the producer has documented and passed all the standards set by its particular certifying association when it comes to the growing, processing, packaging, storing, and shipping of its product, complete with occasional on-site inspection. The certification is meant to prevent fraud and assure that the producer has adhered to a clear set of rules.

Without the certification, anything labelled simply "organic" means you are relying on the word of whoever is calling it that. No one has inspected the farm or production facility and the food producer hasn't necessarily followed all the regulations established by a certifying body. Different jurisdictions have different certifying bodies and each body may have slightly different definitions as to exactly what they consider organic. For Vancouver Island and the Gulf Islands, the Certified Organic Associations of BC (COABC) accredits the Islands Organic Producers Association (IOPA). Farmers and food producers who declare that their products are certified organic should be able to produce the paperwork that proves it. If a producer claims that what he or she is selling is organic, or organically grown or produced, that could mean almost anything unless they have the certification to back it up. Transitional organic means that a product is partway through the process of becoming certified organic, which takes three years.

Biodynamic: Proponents of biodynamic farms and products believe this method of food production is superior to certified organic (or some would say "beyond organic") because it pays more attention to soil, considering it to be one of the living organisms on a farm that must be nurtured and cared for along with the plants and animals. The method emphasizes the use of fermented compost and manures, planting and sowing crops according to the phases of the moon, and land use integration on the farm consisting of crop management, raising livestock, and the overall care of the land. Certification of biodynamic farms is handled in Canada by the Demeter Association.

Free-run, free-range: Neither of these terms guarantees a product that may be healthier for you, the animals involved, or the environment. You see these claims most often on egg cartons and sometimes on meat and poultry packaging. Sustainable-food proponents look for free-run or free-range labels, since many of the eggs we eat are still produced by battery hens in small cages. Up to seven birds are crammed into each fifty-by-sixty-centimetre cage. The cages are just thirty-five centimetres tall and are stacked two to eight cages high; as many as four hundred thousand birds can be kept in one dimly lit barn. The birds suffer from feather loss and weakened bone structure and have their beaks removed to help prevent pecking injuries and cannibalism. The overall environment is also at risk, because of the amount of manure and ammonia gas produced by these chickens living in such a concentrated space. Free-run means the animal is not living in a cage, but this is not a measurable standard and the animal may still live in a crowded barn. Free-range means they have access to outdoors, but again, this is not a measurable standard. Free-range does not equal organic. In BC, COABC regulations mandate that certified organic eggs come from chickens that spend at least one third of their lives outdoors. Why should you take the trouble to find high-quality eggs from a reliable source? First, improved animal welfare, and second, eggs from chickens that are certified organic and free-range are less likely to contain dangerous bacteria such as salmonella, and they are much more nutritious than commercially produced eggs.

Grain-fed, grain-finished, grass-fed, grass-finished, pasture-raised: Most of these terms apply to beef and other protein sources like chicken, pork, and lamb. Grain is often fed to cows raised for beef; it fattens them quickly and develops the "marbling" of fat in choicer cuts. Some people like that marbling and the taste of the fat, but it comes at a price, since many cows spend at least forty-five days in Concentrated Animal Feeding Operations (CAFOs). The animals are crowded into vegetation-less pens (in the case of cattle, a large CAFO is at least one thousand animals) and fed unnatural diets until they are sent to slaughter in order to produce the largest amount of animal protein at the least cost to farmers. Unfortunately, this method also increases the risk of spreading dangerous *E. coli* bacteria and creates waste disposal problems, not to mention a huge amount of methane gas from the belching cows, whose stomachs are not designed to process grain.

"Finishing" an animal means selecting its diet for the 90 to 120 days before slaughter. Grain-finished means the animals may have been raised on pasture but fattened before slaughter on grain, although not necessarily in a CAFO. You may also see "grain-supplemented" on a label for beef, which may mean the grain fed to the cattle was in small amounts so that the animal wasn't sickened by it. Grass-fed and pasture-raised mean the animals spend their lives in pastures, eating grasses. Grass-finished means the animals ate only grasses and hay leading up to slaughter. This is another case in which it benefits you to do some research and ask questions of the butcher or farmer from whom you are buying your beef. To me, grass-fed beef has a much more "beefy" flavour and the side benefit of having higher levels of omega-3 fatty acids and more vitamin E, beta carotene, and vitamin C than CAFO beef. Grass-fed beef and lamb also have less saturated fat, cholesterol, and calories.

Pasture-raised chickens are kept outside in uncrowded bottomless cages that are moved down the pasture on a daily basis. The chickens eat the grass and bugs and leave behind their rich droppings to fertilize the pasture as it regrows in time for the next cycle of chickens.

When you are trying to live a more sustainable lifestyle, cost is also a factor. Certified organic, sustainable, and small-scale products are quite often more expensive than their mass-produced counterparts. Some of your eating lifestyle will depend on your economic situation. I've tried to learn how to do more with less. Because the grass-fed beef I buy is so flavourful, I'm satisfied with eating half the amount I used to. Some people choose to buy certified organic fruits and vegetables to replace the "Dirty Dozen," products deemed to have the highest amounts of pesticide residues by the Environmental Working Group. Apples, strawberries, and celery are among the Dirty Dozen. The price differential is dropping, however, and it's great to see certified organic produce sections in grocery stores growing because of the demand; on any given day you may find a certified organic product that costs less than its conventional counterpart. I'm thankful my mom taught me how to be a thrifty shopper so I pick and choose where to spend my food budget in the most sustainable fashion for me.

The reality is there is no one answer, and it may seem like hard work to make the right choices for you and your family. But look at it this way: part of the homework is getting out and meeting new people like the farmers who grow great ingredients and the artisans who make great products such as cheese and preserves and cured meats. Try these products cooked for you in local restaurants and from food carts, and then buy them at farmers' markets and cook them at home for you and your family. As we move toward a more sustainable food-producing environment, you will meet more and more people who are just as committed to fresh local flavours and healthy foods as you are. And that's not such a bad bit of homework after all . . .

saison
MARKET VINEYARD

Asiago Cheese & Black Pepper
French Bread

$4.75

Just one of the specialty breads at Saison Market Vineyard

BAKERIES

When I was a kid, my mom would go to a variety of supermarkets on Thursday mornings (the sale flyers came in the paper on Wednesday), and in each store she would cruise by the bakery section and pick out whatever bread or buns were in the "reduced for quick sale" bin. We all ate it at home, as toast, in sandwiches, or eventually as breadcrumbs. I guess price overruled quality of the bread. When I left home and met partners who were more serious about bread, I started to pay attention to it. While living in Terrace, I came to treasure Kitwanga bread, sprouted-wheat bread made with care at a Seventh Day Adventist colony called Fairhaven Farm near the small town of Kitwanga, about an hour's drive from Terrace. Eventually I learned how to make my own bread, which I still do from time to time; however, with excellent bakeries to choose from around my home or in Victoria, there really isn't much incentive, since they all do a better job on bread than I do. I've subjected most of the following bakeries to my "croissant test" as well. For me, a perfect croissant is very flaky and crisp on the outside, with lots of moist layers of buttery goodness on the inside. Bread and baked goods are very subjective topics for most serious eaters; you may not agree with all of my choices here, and chances are I've definitely left a few of the best ones out of this edition, so please let me know where they are and why I should visit them in the near future!

HONEY OAT
TRIANGLE

KOULOURIA

The honey oat triangles from **Denman Bakery** are irresistible!

DENMAN BAKERY—COURTENAY

Although Bill Marler had owned the Denman Bakery for thirteen years, he had actually been living for a while in Courtenay. Going back and forth on the ferry to Denman Island every day just didn't make financial sense anymore and was really eating into his time. With most of his wholesale business to Vancouver Island restaurants and shops, a lease running out, and a space well suited for a bakery available just a short walk down the street from his house, deciding to move the business to Courtenay was easy. He still delivers breads and pizzas to Denman four or five times a week. This bakery has built up a loyal following over the years with high-quality sandwich breads, nothing too far outside the box. There are a few specialties, though, including the "take and bake" pizza. You phone in your order. They build it for you from scratch, on its own baking sheet. You pick it up, you put it in the oven, and you never ever have cold pizza. Then there are the triangles, their version of the granola bar. They are a hefty snack; you could make one last a long time, but I have a hard time stopping at one or two bites. You may hear people talking about this bakery by two different names. The sign outside on Fifth Street says DENMAN BAKERY PRESENTS VASSILI'S BREAD SHOP. Bill loves Greece and visits it often. His nickname there is Vassili, so Vassili's it is.

FOL EPI—VICTORIA

My first encounter with Cliff Leir of Fol Epi dates back to 2004. I met him while he was toiling away at Wild Fire Bakery, getting ready to install an on-site mill that would help him grind forthcoming shipments of Red Fife wheat from one particular farmer in Saskatchewan. Those were heady days for Leir, who had gone from selling loaves baked in a self-built wood-fired oven in his driveway to being the main baker champion of Red Fife; he was trying to make sure this heritage variety of wheat, the granddaddy of many modern strains of wheat in Canada, wasn't going to fade into extinction. He told me how it was the best-tasting wheat he'd found so far, with a subtle but definitely much deeper, fuller wheat flavour. He was on to something. Red Fife made a comeback, and Cliff is still using it to bake some of his loaves at Fol Epi, which has grown into more of a full-service establishment offering pizzas, pastries, sandwiches, coffee, etc.

FRY'S RED WHEAT BREAD—VICTORIA

Byron Fry was meant to bake bread. It's in his blood. His great-great-grandfather baked bread in Victoria at the turn of the twentieth century, and when Byron decided to bake bread in Victoria, the space on Craigflower Road that matched his needs was right across the street from the bakery operated by his ancestor all those years ago. Byron's present-day bakery probably doesn't look that much different from the previous incarnation, from the chipped-paint, old-style chairs outside on the sidewalk to the wooden shelves holding the day's baking to the wood-fired brick oven. It was just built in 2012, but the bricks above the oven door already show a soot-stained patina from the thousands of loaves and pastries it has baked so far. Byron's breads are rustic and hearty, but his croissants and *pain au chocolat* pass my flakiness test, and people line up on Sundays for pizza day, featuring toppings of Moss Street Market veggies and Natural Pastures' water buffalo mozzarella.

Frédéric Desbiens, Saison Market Vineyard

Merridale Cidery's Brick Oven Bakery in Cobble Hill produces a
fine array of breads, which are for sale in the ciderhouse.

"The Bread Lady" breads, Salt Spring Island

SAISON MARKET VINEYARD—NORTH COWICHAN

The happy circumstance that brought Saison to North Cowichan began several years ago when baker Ingrid Lehwald was running the very successful Fieldstone Bakery in White Rock and Frédéric Desbiens became her first wholesale customer via his restaurant there. Romance and partnership led them to the Cowichan Valley, where Ingrid grew up.

Their "child," Saison, is a very comfy café and bakery open only on weekends, with a wonderful view of their grapevine-covered property, where you can buy Ingrid's excellent breads and Frédéric's sweet and savoury specialties. My favourites are Frédéric's cherry frangipane tarts, or a slice of Ingrid's bread slathered with their rhubarb and vanilla preserve. The main business of their property is grape growing. Frédéric also has a background in vineyard management. While the grape production is coming along, there is lots to keep them busy at the café, where they try to use the best of local and seasonal ingredients. So they work Thursday, Friday, Saturday, and Sunday in the bakery and café, then Monday, Tuesday, and Wednesday in the vineyard. Frédéric says it's work he loves. "Yes, we have to rush around and work hard to get ready for the weekend, but then early in the week when you are out in the vineyard with the fresh air and a different pace, you slow down and make sure you have your lunch, and you love it even though it is a lot of work."

SALT SPRING BREAD COMPANY—SALT SPRING ISLAND

I don't think anyone actually uses the name Salt Spring Bread Company. To tell you the truth, I had never heard the name before I sat down to write about "The Bread Lady." That is how everyone refers to Heather Campbell, who has been baking marvellous breads on Salt Spring since 1994. You can always find her at the Salt Spring Saturday Market, but if you are on Salt Spring during the week, you really must go to the property where she lives with her architect husband, Phillip Van Horn, who designed the modern yet rustic house they live in with the spectacular view of Swanson Channel between Salt Spring and Pender Islands. You'll also find the studio that houses her large, custom-built wood-burning oven. There is something deeply satisfying about the loaves Heather creates that is hard to describe. Somewhere between the welcome chewiness of the dough and the spark of locally sourced vegetables she stuffs into some of her loaves is a taste only an artisan can create.

TRUE GRAIN BREAD—COWICHAN BAY

About a year after I moved to Cobble Hill, this bakery opened in nearby Cowichan Bay and was the saviour for all bread connoisseurs. Jonathan Knight was the young baker who moved here to pursue his dream of producing artisan and organic breads made the old-fashioned way: no preservatives, dough conditioners, or anything artificial, long fermentations and risings, and texture and flavour to die for. Jonathan quickly built a loyal following, me included, who stopped there every Saturday for a French or sourdough baguette and a loaf of multigrain or perhaps raisin bread. There are seasonal treats—strawberry and raspberry Danishes in the summer, pumpkin-coloured and -shaped challah bread in the fall, and at Christmastime the shortbreads, stollen, and special European-style cookies and pastries that are regular features on many holiday tables. Jonathan ended up with a little more excitement and pace than he wanted, due

True Grain Bread founder Jonathan Knight

True Grain baguettes pair well with freshly cooked crab dipped in melted butter.

to the bakery's popularity, and decamped for life on a farm in northern British Columbia. Bruce and Leslie Stewart took over in 2007 and have stayed true to Jonathan's philosophy of artisan bread with some modern sustainability improvements. There are no plastic bags at the bakery, all takeout packaging is compostable, and the Stewarts purchase as many local ingredients as possible, including eggs and even grain, which is milled on-site (you can watch the big German mill grinding away through a large window). Bruce is quite proud of sometimes being able to sell a "5-mile loaf" when the Red Fife wheat, a heritage variety, is grown at a local farm, or the "35-mile loaf" when it is grown on a farm in Metchosin.

WELL-BRED—CHEMAINUS

Mark Primmer's business card reads WELL-BRED. WELL-READ. WELL-FED. I can't argue with any of that. As long as you accept the pun in bred for bread, you'll be okay. You see, while Mark does make good bread, he is also well-read, having graduated from the University of Alberta with a major in English. I see Mark most Saturday mornings at the Duncan Farmer's Market as he and his wife, Shannon, deal with the usual lineup of customers willing and waiting to buy his breads and pastries. These are produced in his twenty-eight-square-metre former art studio in Chemainus, equipped with a vintage 1952 Hobart mixer. He doesn't have a storefront; he just works full-time to sell his products Saturday morning in Duncan and at the Wednesday market in Chemainus. How he got into baking is a long story, but after a less-than-stellar career in other jobs and a somewhat successful stint at playing the stock market, he is now doing exactly what he wants to do: baking great-tasting breads and pastries and having fun with words and language. So one of his loaves is called The Flaming Fig, and the other day he was making Bacon Killer Brownies. Then there is his Loosely Muesli, and Lemon Trollop instead of the more mundane Lemon Tart. At the end of all the puns and witty repartee at his stand (and on his Facebook page), the important part for me is at the end of his motto—well-fed.

YOU MIGHT ALSO WANT TO TRY:
ITALIAN BAKERY—VICTORIA

Traditional Italian baked goods and pastries and much more. Don't forget to try the panettone around Christmastime.

MERRIDALE ESTATE CIDERY BRICK
OVEN BAKERY—COBBLE HILL

The breads here are leavened with the yeast used in fermenting the apple cider and baked in one of two brick ovens behind the ciderhouse.

WILD FIRE BAKERY—VICTORIA

A family-owned business since 1998, it's in a brightly painted building on the corner of Quadra and Mason. Artisan breads and pastries, and lunches as well!

Peter Kimmerly, Island Spirits Distillery, pours one of his Phrogs.

BEVERAGES AND
SPECIALTY LIQUIDS

While I am trying to give everyone reading this book a good overall sense of this region's artisan products, wine and beer producers have been well covered in other books by other experts in the field. Suffice to say that we have an ever-growing number of specialists here and it is one of the more exciting areas to explore in terms of high quality. Some of the following products contain alcohol, others do not, and some of them are liquids that you don't really drink, as in the case of the Venturi-Schulze vinegar and verjus. The good news is that for people who are interested in tasting (or making) specialty spirits, the provincial government has been making moves over the past few years to change or eliminate some of the archaic laws that have been in place for decades (their only seeming purpose having been to discourage artisans from actually being able to make money in the alcohol end of the business). So in this section you will find listings for some of the more intriguing companies I've visited in my years here on the island and Gulf Islands; they may offer more than just beverages, so look for those products on their websites or in my "You Might Also Want to Try" notes.

BIGLEAF MAPLE SYRUP—VARIOUS LOCATIONS

Back in 2008, on a blustery, damp day, I attended the first-ever Bigleaf Maple Syrup Festival at the Forest Discovery Centre in Duncan.

Organizers were hoping a few hundred people would show up. Nearly fifteen hundred did! It was a major breakthrough for a product that remains a rare find. Attendees learned how to tap their own bigleaf maple trees if they want to try making syrup, watched the sap being boiled down in a wood-fired evaporator, and, of course, got to taste and purchase samples of locally made maple syrup. That year I was honoured to be a judge in the syrup-making competition. I tasted fifteen different syrups and was very pleased to report that I would put the flavour of the winning syrup up against anything I've tasted from eastern Canada. I've judged a few more competitions since then, with the number of entries climbing to over thirty one year. The good news is that the quality of the syrup—from flavour to clarity to viscosity—continues to improve. The bad news is that the demand for this syrup far exceeds the supply. Most artisans are doing it as a hobby, but a few have invested in the equipment necessary to make syrup on a commercial basis. The best time of year to buy it is just as it is made; your best chance is to go to the Bigleaf Maple Syrup Festival held each February at the Forest Discovery Centre in Duncan (www.bcforestdiscoverycentre.com).

BLUE MOON ESTATE WINERY—COURTENAY

People may know the Blue Moon Estate Winery better as the Natures Way Farm, where they go to purchase certified organic blueberries and other fruits and veggies in season. But they would be remiss if they didn't belly up to the tasting bar in the farm-gate shop for a sip of fruit wine. Fruit wines sometimes get a deservedly bad rap. They can be horrible, especially in the hands of amateurs like your Uncle Louie. But the quality of fruit wines and liqueurs from Vancouver Island has been improving to award-winning levels. This is very apparent at Blue Moon. Instead

YOU MIGHT ALSO WANT TO TRY:
CHERRY POINT ESTATE WINES—COBBLE HILL
Although this winery primarily offers wines made with grapes, one of its best-known products is its award-winning Solera Blackberry.

Blueberries from Blue Moon Estate Winery are transformed into award-winning Dusk wine.

of doing something obvious, like making jams or jellies, farmer, wine-maker, and engineer-by-trade George Ehrler decided to get a little bit more serious with the winemaking hobby he had pursued for years. So he built a winery attached to the farm-gate store. George turns blueber-ries, blackberries, apples, and strawberries from the farm into fruit wines and also purchases fruits like pears and cherries from nearby orchards to make into wines. One not to miss is Eclipse, a port-style wine made from Natures Way blueberries and island blackberries. George likes to keep the production small so he can meet potential customers coming in the door. "Our biggest hurdle is getting over the memories people have of the fruit wine their elders used to make down in the basement, and how they didn't really enjoy it. But we have people coming in here now and tasting and saying how it's different than what they remember, and they like it."

ISLAND SODAWORKS—ERRINGTON

It's been a long time since I've drunk anything out of a "stubby" bottle, those brown bottles that used to be the bottle shape for 95 percent of

Cowichan Sunset

Serves 1

This is my wife Ramona's take on a Tequila Sunrise, leaving out the traditional grenadine and using an island blackberry port-style wine instead.

1½ oz (45 mL) tequila
2 oz (60 mL) freshly squeezed orange juice
1 Tbsp (15 mL) Cherry Point Solera or other blackberry dessert wine
orange slice for garnish
soda water or sparkling wine (optional)

Fill a stemmed wine glass with ice and then add the tequila and orange juice. Slowly add the blackberry dessert wine and it will layer its way down through the drink in sunset fashion. Garnish with orange slice. To add a little fizz to the cocktail, fill with either soda water or sparkling wine.

Canadian-made beer. But when I took my first swig of naturally fermented and slightly fizzy pickled-ginger and lemon soda, I was cheering the return of the stubby. The slightly vinegary concoction was sharp and refreshing, and rescued me at the end of a very hot day in Parksville. At the Parksville Summer by the Sea Market I met Mandolyn Jonasson with her wild array of creative beverages, sold in those stubby brown bottles from her Island SodaWorks company (www.facebook.com/IslandSodaWorks). This is soda like you've never had it before. Mandolyn takes all-natural ingredients, ranging anywhere from pickled Japanese plums to rose petals to dandelions, and ferments them in the bottle, creating a low-sugar, good-for-your-gut, tasty beverage. While her company is relatively new, the concept is old. We're talking the Middle Ages here. It's not surprising she had to jump through several regulatory hoops to get the provincial authorization necessary to sell her product. But since she did get the approval, the company has been bubbling along and demand has been growing. It's a hard sell at first; as I watched Mandolyn in action at the market, she had to do quite a bit of explaining to people, describing exactly what her product is and how it is made. "Once I have them, though, they're hooked. Repeat customers are

Cowichan Sunset cocktail (recipe opposite)

Fermented beverages from Island SodaWorks are a throwback to the way many sodas used to be made.

very loyal, and it's funny how some of my older customers remember these kinds of drinks from the past. One woman swears by my sodas to help her digestive system." Bartenders (or mixologists) are also creating cocktails using Mandolyn's sodas as a base. Flavours change with the season and the availability of local fruits and vegetables, but look for this natural beverage to start making a dent in the popularity of those ubiquitous, big-bubbled, high-fructose corn-syrup pops.

PHILLIPS SODA WORKS—VICTORIA

Sparkmouth ginger ale and Captain Electro's Intergalactic root beer are the first two products coming out of this subsidiary of Phillips Brewing. I get only an occasional craving for root beer, but I have to toast Captain Electro for his Intergalactic Root Beer. It tastes smooth and rich, not at all harsh like more commercially produced sodas. The Sparkmouth Ginger Ale has a very zingy, upfront ginger flavour.

ISLAND SPIRITS DISTILLERY—HORNBY ISLAND

It's difficult to "distill" the "spirit" you get when you hit the entranceway of this distillery on Hornby Island. After driving through the dense bush lining the gravel road, you come to a clearing and the cedar-shake-clad home of the Phrog line of spirits. The modest footprint of the distillery is a pleasant reminder of when spirits were distilled by small companies around the country instead of in today's massive factories, where speed and quantity, rather than patience and quality, rule. Peter Kimmerly, John Grayson, and Dr. Naz Abdurahman teamed up in the early 2000s to share their love of experimenting with distilling spirits, and their products win rave reviews from consumers and at tasting competitions. Their Phrog gin and Phrog vodka are named to celebrate the multitudes of singing frogs on the Hornby property; the "Ph" reflects the scientific nature of the trio, pH being the measure used to describe the level of acidity in a substance. I have sat at the comfortable tasting counter, admired the complex curves of the still, marvelled at the number of aromatic botanicals added to the Phrog gin, such as juniper, coriander, cinnamon, and eleven more, and then sipped and relaxed. The vodka is very smooth. The gin changes with every sip, more of the aromatics being released as you swirl it in your mouth and expose it to air.

MERRIDALE ESTATE CIDERY—COBBLE HILL

When I first met Rick Pipes and Janet Docherty of Merridale Cidery, this husband-and-wife team was still experiencing the growing pains of purchasing an old cidery that, as the realtors probably put it, "has lots of potential." One day I arrived during a cider apple "crush" day, when Rick was practising new-found electrical skills in repairing a finicky switch,

YOU MIGHT ALSO WANT TO TRY: ORGANIC FAIR SODA SYRUPS—COBBLE HILL

Organic Fair creates a variety of syrups available in funky, old-style medicine bottles. They're made from organic fair-trade cane sugar, their own spring water, herbs grown in their gardens, and other natural ingredients. Flavours include Root Beer, Ginger Ale, Vanilla Rhubarb, and Lavender Lemon Balm Lemonaid. Just measure the syrups into a glass and add your own carbonated water.

The Brandy House at Merridale Estate Cidery, BC's first craft distillery

then used an old hockey stick to stickhandle apples up a rickety conveyor belt to the press, where old sheets of canvas, valued for their natural stores of beneficial yeasts, could rip apart at any time as they filtered the juice from the pressed apples. Things have changed a little since then, as the dynamic duo has pushed ahead with project after project for the cidery, which is so popular it gets about thirty thousand visitors each year. There are the bistro, the outdoor cookhouse and patio with wood-burning brick oven and smoker, the tasting room, the deli and gift shop featuring local art, crafts, and food items, including baked goods from that brick oven and house-cured meats, and the perfect wedding gazebo, overlooking a peaceful pond with the nearby apple orchard bobbing in fruit. And then there is the Brandy House. In June of 2013 Merridale obtained the first artisan distiller's licence in the province, a breakthrough in provincial liquor legislation that makes it possible for smaller distilleries to actually make a profit on their products. Rick is especially proud of his apple and pear brandies, and he should be. They taste as good as anything made in the time-honoured European tradition.

Specialty pear cider from Sea Cider Farm and Ciderhouse

SEA CIDER FARM AND CIDERHOUSE—SAANICHTON

There aren't a lot of companies making authentic fruit ciders in British Columbia, but with companies like Merridale and Sea Cider leading the resurgence in crafting unique blends, this old beverage will gain new fans. I think our palates are becoming much more sophisticated now, and more people are looking for different taste experiences. Kristen Jordan at Sea Cider has persisted in marketing the image of cider as a sophisticated beverage and it shows, not only in the taste of her products but also in the packaging, the decor of the ciderhouse, and the knowledge and professionalism of her staff. There are a couple of products of note. The Rumrunner cider is crafted from local heritage apples and then aged in rum barrels. If you visit, ask about Kristen's adventure in getting the barrels. And then there is the Kings and Spies cider, made mostly from King and Northern Spy apples gleaned from backyards in Victoria by LifeCycles, a local food security agency. Proceeds from the sales of Kings and Spies go toward supporting LifeCycles. It's great to see fruit that would otherwise be wasted go to a good cause. In another "don't waste it, use it" scenario, a former cidermaker at Sea Cider took advantage of the discovery of an abandoned orchard in the area that had "perry" pear trees, decades-old trees that prove that pear cider, or perry, was once produced on Vancouver Island. When the cidermaker first tasted them, they were so astringent that just a tiny piece completely dried out his mouth. Of the two varieties harvested, both were small, about the size of limes. The only reason for planting these trees would have been to make perry from the fruit. The Sea Cider perry is a limited-edition, seasonal product. Check at the cidery in the spring. If you're lucky, you just might be able to taste a very rare island artisan product.

SHELTER POINT DISTILLERY— CAMPBELL RIVER

When you start out wanting to make a single malt whisky on Vancouver Island using Vancouver Island grain, you need two things: time and money. Both of these factors are amply on display at the Shelter Point Distillery, located on a beautiful piece of farmland with an impeccable water supply just south of Campbell River. The money spent on the infrastructure is evident from the moment you walk into the distillery and observe the beautiful woodwork, the etched glass showing the story of distilling from the grainfields to the glass, and the truly magnificent copper stills imported from Scotland. The time comes in the form of a Canadian law that states whisky cannot be called whisky until it has been aged in a used oak barrel for three years and a day; 2014 will mark the first year that Shelter Point whisky can be called whisky. In 2013 I was lucky enough to taste a sample of the soon-to-be-whisky direct from one of the oak barrels, and I can report that it will be worth every penny spent and every second ticked by. Shelter Point is also offering other products crafted from the farm around the distillery, such as fruit-based liqueurs and vodka.

SPINNAKERS GASTRO BREWPUB—VICTORIA

I have a penchant for things that are vinegary in nature. At any given time you will find at least half a dozen different types of vinegar in a tall drawer in my kitchen. One of those vinegars is usually a malt vinegar

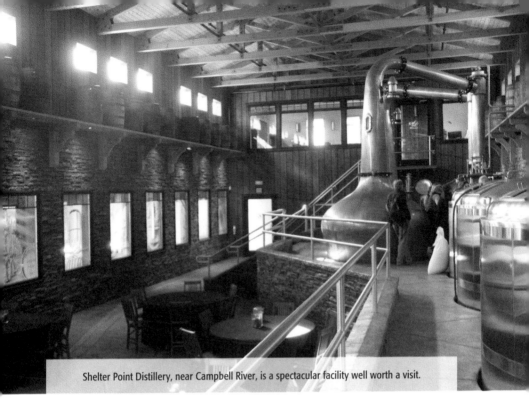

Shelter Point Distillery, near Campbell River, is a spectacular facility well worth a visit.

from Spinnakers Gastro Brewpub. Of course, Spinnakers is well known for its beer and was one of the first brewpubs licensed in BC, ushering in the new age of craft beer in the mid-1980s. Some of the beers brewed in Spinnakers' stainless-steel tanks are encouraged to turn to vinegar and then are placed in oak barrels to carefully age for several months in the craft tradition. Commercial vinegars are merely acetic acid with some caramel colouring added to give the appearance of an aged vinegar, but they taste sharp and crude. Why buy that when you can get the real stuff? Now, it may be that you have visited Spinnakers just to get some vinegar, but I recommend trying the Cask of the Day at the bar, maybe some BC mussels steamed in ale from the menu, and a lengthy browse at the Spinnakers provisions store near the entrance to the pub. There you will find a wide selection of vinegars, along with house-made, beer-based mustards, breads, baked goods and pastries, other beer-based condiments, and even chocolate truffles, as well as items from other artisans mentioned in this book, such as the Vancouver Island Salt Company and Salt Spring Island Cheese.

Tugwell Creek Honey Farm and Meadery—near Sooke

Mead comes from honey, which comes from honeybees. Bob Liptrot of Tugwell was almost born into beekeeping. He started learning about bees and honey when he was six years old in East Vancouver. "When I was in grade school, I used to walk back and forth to school past a neighbour who was a beekeeper. He was an old Scotsman who knew the value of free help, so he would get me to help him, and if I was lucky, he would give me a piece of honeycomb to eat. I was scraping hives, painting them, getting them ready for the next season, extracting honey, filling jars." Bob really "got the bug," so to speak, and embarked on a career as an entomologist; he always kept bees as a hobby until he and his wife decided to move to Vancouver Island to set up the farm at Tugwell Creek. Fermented honey makes mead, and it was a natural progression for Bob, having all that honey around, to start experimenting with mead. He's been very successful in developing a nice line of meads, just as a winemaker develops different products from his grapes. The recipe for one, the Wassail Gold, goes back to the mid-1500s. In addition to honey, the wassail contains six different spices. The Dutch East India Company created the recipe when it was trying to promote the use of spices in Europe, and at the time, only the aristocracy could afford it. You can probably afford the drive past Sooke to Tugwell Creek, where you can watch Bob tending his beehives and taste the range of his meads, which are also available at shops and restaurants on the island and the Lower Mainland.

Venturi-Schulze Vineyards—Cobble Hill

Giordano Venturi and Marilyn Schulze moved to the Cowichan Valley in 1987, and since then, they and Marilyn's daughter, Michelle, have become well known for wines grown from grapes that are carefully selected for their unique microclimate and *terroir*. But you absolutely have to try their balsamic vinegar. It is made according to the tradition established hundreds of years ago in north-central Italy, in places like Modena and Reggio Emilia. True balsamic vinegar is made from grape must reduced over an open fire, then aged for years and years in a series

Verjus Sorbet
Makes about 2½ cups (625 mL)

Yet another use for verjus is offered here by the Venturi-Schulzes. They describe this as "Totally yummy!" This would be great served as a palate cleanser between courses of a meal or as a very simple dessert with some fresh fruit or even frozen grapes. The recipe can be doubled or tripled.

1 bottle (375 mL) Venturi-Schulze verjus
¾ cup (175 mL) simple syrup (see below)
½ tsp (2 mL) finely grated or minced lemon or grapefruit peel
  (optional)

For a sorbet ready within 25 minutes, start with verjus and simple syrup that are well chilled. Add the lemon or grapefruit peel and stir together until well mixed. Process in an ice-cream maker as per manufacturer's directions.

If a more tart sorbet is desired, start with ½ cup of simple syrup. You can add additional simple syrup a bit at a time to your taste, keeping in mind that when frozen, the sorbet will become sharper.

If you don't have an ice-cream maker, make the sorbet a day ahead. Put the mixture in a shallow pan in the freezer. Every half hour or hour, drag a fork through the mixture to break up the ice crystals as they form. When it's completely frozen, process with a mixer, food processor, or blender to a fine consistency and freeze in an airtight container.

Simple Syrup: Dissolve 1 cup (250 mL) of sugar in 1 cup (250 mL) of boiling water. Chill before using in the sorbet recipe and store unused syrup in the refrigerator.

of special barrels made from different kinds of aromatic woods. A bottle of V-S balsamic vinegar is costly, no doubt about that, but I firmly believe it's worth it. The flavour is like nothing else you've tasted. A great deal of labour goes into growing the grapes; then there is the cost of the barrels, imported from Italy, and the time it takes before they have an authentic balsamic vinegar they can bottle, at least four to six years. Those "authentic" balsamic vinegars you can buy for five bucks

Barrels used to age traditional balsamic vinegar at Venturi-Schulze Vineyards are imported from Italy and made from acacia, cherry, ash, oak, and chestnut.

a bottle at the supermarket these days are industrial products. They are made in Italy, according to standards, but the grapes are not organically grown; companies could make it overnight by quickly souring some alcohol and then adding colourings, sugars, and flavours. NOT a traditional method.

Another Venturi-Schulze product that's not quite so expensive is verjus, only twelve dollars for a 375-millilitre bottle. *Verjus* literally translates from the French as "green juice." Marilyn explains, "In our vineyard we thin out a lot of unripe grapes, and it seemed such a shame to just let them fall to the ground, so we started to collect them and crush them to make our own verjus, which we pasteurize and bottle." You can use verjus in your cooking to liven up a sauce or add it to cocktails or just to soda water for a nice little spritzer. It's tart, sweet, and refreshing all at the same time.

Balsamic vinegar from Venturi-Schulze Vineyards

Cured meats hanging at the Whole Beast Salumeria

BUTCHERS, CHARCUTIERS, AND SALUMISTS

Everyone knows what to find at a butcher shop and what butchers do. They take whole animals and cut them into more manageable pieces for the home cook: steaks, chops, chicken breasts, and so on. But you may be less familiar with the somewhat strange-sounding *charcuterie* and *salumi*. Charcuterie is a French term (*char* for "sear" and *cuite* for "cooked") for meats (traditionally pork) that have been cooked, cured, or preserved in some way; charcuterie could be something like a chicken pot pie, a fresh sausage, or a complex terrine of *foie gras* stuffed with truffles and baked in a rich pastry. A shop selling these products is also called a charcuterie, while the person performing this art is a *charcutier*. *Salumi* is an Italian term for cured meat, so a salumist is a person who makes salumi. Salumi includes prosciutto, salami, and pancetta as well as cured sausages, which are infinite in their variations. The best news is that we have a mix of traditionalists and newcomers to the art in this region, making products that in some instances mirror their roots in Europe and in others add regional twists. Don't be afraid to try things like blood sausage or *guanciale* (cured pork jowl); otherwise you'll be missing out on new flavours and textures. Butchers, charcutiers, and salumists are "in" professions these days. We lost many small, privately owned firms as the general population started shopping in supermarkets, where most of the butchery is done in a centrally located distribution facility. That trend is reversing as more people demand to know where their meat comes from and ask for more local products. The following shops not only create products for sale in the store but also prepare goods for other shops and restaurants.

CHOUX CHOUX CHARCUTERIE—VICTORIA

Partners Luke Young and Paige Symonds opened this shop in 2005, filling an empty hole in the middle of the city's Antique Row on Fort Street. It may have stood out like a sore thumb, but I overheard some patrons in those early days say they had been waiting for a European-style deli like this in Victoria for the past thirty or forty years! The wait was worth it then and still is now if you have to bide your time at the counter when the shop is filled with patrons. As young first-time business owners, Luke and Paige were a little overwhelmed with their early success, but they have grown into accomplished artisans, turning out rillettes, terrines, and pâtés in an authentic French style. I love their fresh Merguez sausage and rabbit terrine. Great for takeout but also a super place to stop for lunch with their daily plats du jour.

COWICHAN VALLEY MEAT MARKET—SOUTH OF DUNCAN

This butcher shop is the go-to place for quality and tradition for residents of the Cowichan Valley and also for many customers willing to make the drive over the Malahat. The shop is owned by the Quist family (in the valley since 1923), which supplies the shop from a large farm and abattoir it owns north of Duncan. This is where many of the animals that end up in the butcher shop are raised, on farm-grown forage with no hormones, so it's a great source of local meats, although the retail outlet has been so successful that the Quists do source some of their animals from the British Columbia Interior, raised to their exact specifications. They are always happy to cut a steak or roast just the way you want it and have been working on a growing variety of in-house-cured meats. Even if you're just passing through from up or down island, don't miss picking up a package of their double-smoked bacon. Over the past few years, the

Processing room at Gunter Brothers Meats, a valuable infrastructure asset for the Comox Valley

shop has expanded its line of house-made deli meats and carries a number of other locally made products such as spice rubs from Organic Fair and sea salt from the Vancouver Island Salt Company.

GUNTER BROTHERS MEATS—COURTENAY

Gunter Brothers Meats has been a family-owned and -operated business in the Comox Valley since 1932. While brothers Dennis and Harry Gunter took over from their father in 1987, they can trace their craft back to their grandfather, who founded the company as an on-farm facility when he moved here from England. He learned his trade from his own grandfather, so we are talking five generations. The current processing plant and retail store sits just north of Courtenay, a collection of unassuming green metal-clad buildings. I toured the processing plant a few years ago and was impressed with its collection of modern processing equipment and attention to cleanliness and detail. Once you step inside the retail shop, though, the unmistakable aroma of smoked meat asserts itself and you know you are in a place that takes its art seriously. You'll find a wide selection of fresh, frozen, and cured products along with a smattering of other common deli products like mustards and colourful cans of spices. Where this company really shines is in its service as a slaughterhouse and processor for local livestock farmers. Without this kind of facility, it just wouldn't be possible for them to economically get their products to market.

ISLAND FARMHOUSE POULTRY—COWICHAN BAY

You will find Island Farmhouse Poultry products in more than three dozen of the more independent grocery stores up and down the island, from Campbell River to Sooke. While the distinctive logo on the package immediately tells you the chicken inside was raised and processed on the island, it doesn't give you the story about how the company came to be and why you should be backing a local hero. When the provincial government announced its intention to update meat inspection regulations, the almost immediate result was that a number of companies announced they would be shutting down. They either had no desire or not enough money to make the mandated changes to their operations. For Lyle Young of Cowichan Bay Farm, that meant he would have to ship his pastured chickens and ducks to the Lower Mainland for slaughtering and have them shipped back again for sale. Instead, he decided to build his own processing plant to do his poultry and that of other area farmers. It wasn't easy. As the owner of the first facility to be built under the new regulations, Young became the guinea pig for the interpretation of the new rules and had to alter his blueprints several times. He had to beg the larger processors for a share of their quota and expand production over what he had imagined just to get the operation into the black. Ten years later, Young provides a valuable service to all sizes of poultry farms in the area, employs dozens of local workers, and supplies a high-quality air-chilled product to customers who want to know that the chicken they're cooking and eating was raised on Vancouver Island.

Braised Moroccan Chicken Thighs
Serves 4

I developed this recipe after a Moroccan lamb shank tagine recipe I was fond of, but when big trays of Island Farmhouse Poultry thighs went on sale, I decided to convert it. This is a "put-it-in-the-oven-and-forget-it" dish for the most part and is easily expandable to accommodate a crowd. Preserved lemons are not a must for this dish but add an intriguing flavour. They are available in most Mediterranean or Middle Eastern markets.

8 large chicken thighs, bone in, skin on
salt and freshly ground black pepper to taste
2 Tbsp (30 mL) olive oil
2 preserved lemons, rinsed, each cut into 4 pieces, flesh removed
    and discarded
8 pearl onions or shallots, peeled
4 medium carrots, peeled and cut in half
1 large bulb of fennel, cut into chunks (optional)
8 large cloves garlic, peeled
8 dried apricots
1 cinnamon stick
6 cardamom pods
1 to 2 cups (250 to 500 mL) white wine
1 cup (250 mL) chopped fresh cilantro for garnish

Preheat oven to 350°F (180°C). Season the chicken thighs with salt and pepper. Heat the olive oil over medium-high heat in an ovenproof pot large enough to hold the thighs in one or two layers. Brown the thighs on both sides, then add all the lemon pieces, vegetables, apricots, and spices and enough white wine to cover the thighs. Bring to a boil, then remove from heat, cover the pot, and put it into the preheated oven for 1 hour. Check after 30 minutes to see if you need more wine to keep the chicken and vegetables from drying out. If so, add more wine, or water if preferred. The thighs are done when they are fork-tender and juices running from near the bone are clear. Remove the cinnamon stick and the cardamom pods before serving. Serve in bowls with the juices, on top of couscous (or rice), and sprinkle each bowl with chopped cilantro.

McLennan's Island Meat and Seafood—
Cook Street Village, Victoria

Lloyd McLennan is a ferocious promoter of local meats, poultry, and seafood. Maybe that's why his nickname is "The MEATDOGG." His narrow but packed shop is full of fresh and marinated meats and seafood and local processed food products like Maypenny Farms jams and Phillips sodas. With butchery in his roots, Lloyd believes in preparing products for his customers "just as I would like it for myself" and makes sure all of his staff share his knowledge of the provenance of their products. As we walked along his meat counter, he pointed out Tannadice Farms pork, "but I'm also getting a lot of beef from them, chicken from Island Farmhouse Poultry. The lamb is local as well." He does admit to bringing in some beef from Alberta, but it's from a rancher he knows and there's no other way to keep the higher-end cuts like tenderloins and rib-eyes in stock. Lloyd also makes a great variety of hamburgers and sausages and will do custom work at the drop of a hat. "If a customer happens to be allergic to garlic, I'll make up sausages just for them without garlic or any other ingredient they don't like or can't handle."

Nanaimo Sausage House—Nanaimo

This charcuterie has been in business in Nanaimo for over thirty years. While I'm usually a consumer of French- or Italian-style cured meat and sausages, this place has brought more Eastern European specialties to my plate. Like what? Like this, a reply on their Facebook page to a customer inquiring about their list of goods: "We have our Nanaimo Sausage, a mild and flavourful kielbasa, we have ham sausages, smokies, garlic lovers', honey garlic turkey, all sorts of pepperonis, tasty double-smoked bacon, Landjäger, salamis, a freezer full of fresh sausages. Not to mention all sorts of meat pies, pierogies, cabbage rolls, soups, cheeses, pickled things, chocolate things, etc., etc." Their pork products are all made from hormone-free pigs raised in the Fraser Valley. No fillers, preservatives, or binders are used. They also make some products using Vancouver Island bison! The current owner, Catherine Clarke, and her business partner, Pawel Biegun, were looking for opportunities. Pawel had known the

Just some of the thirty varieties of sausage available at Nanaimo Sausage House

couple who started the Nanaimo Sausage House since he arrived from Poland twenty years ago, so they bought into a successful company from owners who were willing to pass on all of their recipes and methodology. They don't do mail order, but their reputation goes far beyond Nanaimo. It's not unusual for visitors to drop into the shop to pick up a supply of sausage for their family back home in other parts of BC and beyond.

THE WHOLE BEAST ARTISAN SALUMERIA—OAK BAY

I first met the co-owner of the Whole Beast, Cory Pelan, when he was the chef at La Piola restaurant in Victoria. When his contract to run that restaurant was about to end, he was thinking about moving to or starting another restaurant, just as most chefs would. Then he had second thoughts: "I kind of had an epiphany with a pig one afternoon. I was in the kitchen, working with a whole carcass, breaking it down and eventually making maybe fifteen or twenty different products with it, and thinking that this was the happiest I'd been in my working life, so that's when I thought I could do something like this full-time." When some retail and prep space opened up beside Village Butcher in Oak Bay Village, he was ready to make the leap from chef to salumist. During my first visit to the shop, I was really impressed with the variety and quality of the products Cory was able to offer in his first year of operation; there are different kinds of bacon, spicy capicollo, *guanciale*, *lardo*, pork belly confit, *coppa*, pancetta, and more, and a whole line of fresh sausages. There are also house-made preserves that you serve with these products, honey candy cane beets, pickled broccoli, mixed Italian-style pickles, pickled peppers, even Cory's own pickled ginger, which is superior to anything you can buy in a jar. Cory and his partner, Jeff Pinch, rotate a product line of over fifty different items. My favourite so far? Thin slices of dry-cured sausages laced with truffle.

VILLAGE BUTCHER—OAK BAY

There isn't even a wall between the retail space of the Whole Beast Salumeria and Village Butcher. Convenient, that is. While the Whole Beast specializes in curing meats, Village Butcher is your place next door for fresh meats, along with some charcuterie and decadent lunchtime sandwiches as well. Owners Michael Windle and Rebecca Teskey take a lot of care in selecting their beef and other proteins for their customers. They only purchase whole carcasses, as often as possible from Vancouver Island farms. Most of their pork comes from one farmer in Metchosin. Michael does all the lamb slaughtering on South Vancouver Island. So he and Rebecca know the farmers and they know the people who work in the abattoirs; that means their products have a pretty solid traceability. Rebecca told me that the growth at their shop means a chance at continued existence for the small farmers who supply them. Their pig farmer in Metchosin, for example, was able to build new barns and add other infrastructure based on the weekly orders from Village Butcher, and he and another farmer are putting previously fallow Agricultural Land Reserve acreage back into production. You'll pay a little more for your meats here, but once you've tried their chimichurri flank steak grilled and thinly sliced, you will know that it's worth it.

YOU MIGHT ALSO WANT TO TRY:
GALLOPING GOOSE SAUSAGES—METCHOSIN

A perennial winner in public polling, Galloping Goose Sausages makes a wide variety of high-quality sausages, which can be found for sale in some supermarkets and smaller grocery stores.

Cory Pelan of the Whole Beast Artisan Salumeria

Chef Brock Windsor, Stone Soup Inn, Lake Cowichan PHOTO: BETTINA HARVEY

CHEFS AND INSTRUCTORS

I wanted to include a few chefs and cooking-school instructors in this book because they are often the first people to tell us about, or show us, or cook for us, the quality ingredients produced in this region. In a sense they help steer our food culture, as a good chef is always looking for the best ingredients and products to use in his or her cooking, and a good instructor takes the time to explain those ingredients: where to find them, why they like them, and, most important, how to use them. I would also like to credit Sinclair and Frederique Philip of Sooke Harbour House for being an important nurturing factor in the development of many of the fine chefs now working in this part of the province, across Canada, and even around the world. The Philips' unflagging devotion over the past thirty years to serving local and seasonal foods in their restaurant at the inn has shown many chefs how to look not only within the boundaries of their neighbourhoods but right in their own backyards. The following chefs have all worked at Sooke Harbour House at one point in their careers and they've all gone on to reflect the philosophy of what they learned there. I'm sure you will recognize some or most of these names: Sam Benedetto, Andrea Carlson, Pia Carroll, Jonathan Chovancek, Melissa Craig, David Feys, Bill Jones, Michael Stadtlander, Edward Tuson, Rhonda Viani, James Walt, Brock Windsor, and Peter Zambri. There are many more unsung heroes toiling in the kitchens of our food-service establishments, and I urge you to seek out those who give as much care and attention to local ingredients as the chefs noted above.

CHEF HEIDI FINK—INSTRUCTOR, VICTORIA

Heidi Fink (www.chefheidifink.com) first made her name in Vancouver Island culinary circles as the executive chef at Rebar Modern Food Restaurant in Victoria. Since leaving daily restaurant life, she has become one of the most popular cooking-class instructors in the region. You can find her teaching at any number of venues around Victoria and up into the Cowichan Valley. Heidi's clients are effusive in their praise, with remarks on her website such as "her culinary knowledge, creativity and energy make her a wonder to watch in the kitchen."

She hasn't stopped at teaching, though. I love reading her blog, which shares some of her sometimes hilarious stories of family life and many recipes that prove irresistible. It turns out she likes canning as much as I do, and her Facebook postings in the summer and fall include status updates such as "Just picked up 200 pounds of blueberries, hope there's room in the freezer!" Heidi is a frequent contributor to Victoria-based *EAT Magazine* and also leads culinary tours in Victoria's Chinatown. Her specialty is teaching classes in Thai and Indian cuisine, and she loves to let you roll up your sleeves and get right into the kitchen!

CHEF DAN HAYES, THE LONDON CHEF—VICTORIA

When Dan Hayes blew into Victoria from the United Kingdom a few years ago, there was no mistaking his accent and his brand, "The London Chef." While teaching cooking classes in a number of locations, Dan and his wife, Micayla, were keeping their eyes out for a good location for their cooking school. When they found it on Fort Street, they didn't scrimp on the fittings and interior decor. The London Chef is outfitted with a series of cooking stations, each with its own stove, so you can cook along with Dan or the other instructors as they teach you dishes from cuisines around the world. Dan's breezy and comfortable manner is mixed with a steady infusion of information and recipes that are very doable for the home cook. He's a champion of local ingredients and has made it a personal goal to try to get everyone to eat a wider variety of seafood; he laments the fact that we throw so much seafood back into the ocean when we could be chowing down on delicious dishes of dogfish,

Kathy Jerritt's Blackberry Chocolate Brownies
Makes 16 2-inch (5 cm) squares

Whenever I make these brownies I get either requests for the recipe or a plea for me to make more. That's what you call a "keeper" recipe. When Kathy sent me this recipe, she told me, "I love blackberries and dark chocolate together; it's an underrated combo in my opinion! This moist and decadent brownie can be made using fresh or frozen blackberries, and I use Denman Island chocolate for this recipe."

½ cup (125 mL) unsalted butter, melted
⅓ cup (80 mL) white sugar
2 eggs
1 tsp (5 mL) vanilla
⅓ cup (80 mL) unsweetened cocoa powder
½ cup (125 mL) flour
¼ tsp (1 mL) salt
¼ tsp (1 mL) baking powder
⅓ cup (80 mL) finely chopped dark chocolate—must be dark!
1 cup (250 mL) fresh or frozen blackberries

Preheat oven to 350°F (180°C) and grease an 8-inch (20 cm) -square baking pan. Whisk the melted butter and sugar in a bowl and gradually beat in the eggs. Add the vanilla and then stir in the cocoa powder. Add the flour, salt, and baking powder and mix just until all ingredients are well combined. Stir in the chopped chocolate and very gently fold the blackberries into the mixture. Spread the batter evenly in the pan and bake the brownies for 25 to 30 minutes or until a toothpick inserted in the centre comes out clean. Serve with fresh blackberries and a little whipped cream for a truly decadent mid-afternoon treat.

octopus, or mackerel. Along with the cooking school, the London Chef offers a weekday café and pantry stocked with house-made, local, and international foodstuffs, Lunch and Learn specials, a dining room for special events, and catering. There's always something happening there and you'll always pick up on the latest trends in food culture.

Chef Kathy Jerritt of Tria Fine Catering and Gourmet Eats PHOTO: BETTINA HARVEY

CHEF KATHY JERRITT—TRIA FINE CATERING AND GOURMET EATS, COURTENAY

Kathy Jerritt is one of those chefs who makes you wonder if she ever has the time to sleep in between the many projects she has on the go. When I first met her, she was teaching cooking classes at Natures Way Farm in Courtenay, where she also launched the successful summertime Full Moon Feasts, at which diners nosh on many culinary treats in spectacular outdoor locations on the nights of the full moon. Then there are her appearances at the Comox Valley Farmers' Market with her crepe wagon, offering both sweet and savoury crepes loaded with fresh local veggies or fruits. Since leaving Natures Way, Kathy has purchased a full-service catering company that carries on her philosophy of showcasing local foods, just as she does during the Full Moon Feasts and through her other venture of frozen take-home dinners that easily rival what most restaurants could deliver to your table.

CHEF BILL JONES—DEERHOLME FARM, GLENORA

I knew Bill Jones back when he lived in Vancouver, and even then he was teaching people how to cook, developing menus for new restaurants, helping to hire and train cooks for those restaurants, and also turning up at Granville Island week after week to give free cooking demos to shoppers so they could enjoy the best of the season. When he moved to Vancouver Island, it was a loss to the big city. However, it was a big plus for me when I decided to relocate to the island a few years after he and his wife, Lynn, made their exodus. Bill and Lynn found a piece of land with a century-old cabin, which Bill renovated into his kitchen and dining room; there he teaches cooking classes and serves dinners that showcase not only produce from Lynn's garden but ingredients from nearby farms. Bill is also the author of a number of cookbooks, including some about his chief passion, mushrooms. It's no coincidence that his own property yields some of these edible delicacies, and one of the most enjoyable ways to spend a morning in the Cowichan Valley is a stroll with Bill through the forest near his home. He reveals his vast store of knowledge about fungi and other morsels you can forage for, including such delights as oxeye daisy

Chef Bill Jones, Deerholme Farm
PHOTO: STEPHEN HAWKINS

and the young needle tips of grand fir trees. If you're looking to increase your knowledge of local ingredients by learning to identify them, shop for them, or cook them, you don't have to go further than Deerholme Farm in Glenora.

DAVID MINCEY—CIRCLE CANNING AND PRESERVATION FOODS CHOCOLATE PROJECT, VICTORIA

The long-time owner and chef of Camille's Restaurant in Victoria first came to my attention years ago when he was trying to help farmers on the Saanich Peninsula sell directly to restaurants by urging them to grow exactly what the chef wanted. Our first meeting was at Holland Farm, where David, nattily dressed in crisp blue shirt and tie, carefully placed plastic buckets full of fresh veggies into a beat-up pickup truck to take to Camille's kitchen. David is the co-founder of the Island Chefs Collaborative, and back then the ICC helped Holland Farm with a thousand-dollar donation; it enabled the farmers to build fences to keep out hungry deer and install drip irrigation, which saved them hours of time in watering. Corry Matechuk of Holland Farm says that without David's mentoring and support in guiding them in how to grow for restaurants, they likely would have folded operations within a year or two. When David succeeded in picking up more than enough produce from farmers to supply restaurants, he created a market in Bastion Square to sell the excess, and when there were leftovers from that effort, he started canning them and selling them in subsequent weeks. Talk about industrious!

Now David has left the day-to-day hubbub of Camille's and pursues two of his chief fascinations: preserving fresh, seasonal, and local foods through his company, Circle Canning, and chocolate, through his Preservation Foods Chocolate Project (www.camillesrestaurant.com/chocolate). For the canning, David and his wife, Paige, create about fifty different products over the course of a year, purchasing and preserving everything they can get their hands on from local farmers and using some of the recipes he developed over the years of creating condiments for the table at Camille's. To find his products, you'll have to search out Circle Canning at one of many Victoria-area farmers' markets; as

Chef Ronald St. Pierre, Locals Restaurant
PHOTO: STEPHEN HAWKINS

they usually do four to five a week, it shouldn't be too hard. Also, for more than twenty years now, David has been on a mission to discover artisanal manufacturers of bean-to-bar fair-trade chocolate from all over the world. (See Organic Fair, page 58.) He's up to around sixty makers, representing 180 different chocolate bars. He then distributes them to smaller retailers of artisanal foods in Victoria and also leads classes in how to appreciate these fine chocolates. What a sweet business!

CHEF RONALD ST. PIERRE, LOCALS RESTAURANT, COURTENAY

The first thing you see when you walk in the front door of Locals Restaurant is a rack full of business cards. They aren't from travelling salesmen or nearby businesses; they are the business cards of all the different local food suppliers the restaurant uses. Ronald St. Pierre grew up in rural Quebec, where all the ingredients on his family's dinner table came from local farms. When he opened his own restaurant, he saw

Porcini-and-Rice-Flour-Crusted Salmon with Spicy Tomato and Root Vegetable Confit

by Chef Bill Jones, Deerholme Farm

Serves 4

To make the porcini powder called for in this recipe, put a quarter-cup of dried porcini mushrooms in a small coffee or spice grinder and process into a powder. You can also use a mortar and pestle. The ground powder will last for many months. You can also mix it with sea salt to make a porcini-flavoured salt.

For the Confit:
1 cup (250 mL) extra-virgin olive oil
2 cups (500 mL) fingerling (or nugget) potatoes, cut in half
1 bunch baby carrots, washed, trimmed, cut in half
1 whole garlic bulb, separated into cloves and peeled
2 cups (500 mL) cherry or plum tomatoes, cut in half
1 hot chili pepper, split (or more to taste)
small bunch basil leaves

For the Salmon:
4 4-oz (100 g) salmon fillets
salt and pepper to taste
2 Tbsp (30 mL) porcini powder
¼ cup (60 mL) rice flour
oil from confit
good balsamic vinegar
fresh lemon wedge
fresh herbs for garnish, chopped

In a small roasting pan, put the olive oil, potatoes, carrots, and garlic cloves in a single layer. Roast in a 350°F (180°C) oven for 10 minutes, then add the tomatoes, chili, and basil leaves. Bake for an additional 20 to 30 minutes or until the potatoes are tender and the tomatoes are split and just beginning to char. Remove from heat and allow to cool in the pan.

Meanwhile, place the salmon on a plate and season well with salt and pepper. Mix the porcini powder and rice flour and sprinkle this on the salmon. Turn fish repeatedly to coat evenly with the mixture.

Heat a skillet (we use cast iron) over medium-high and add a few spoonfuls of the oil from the confit pan. When it's hot, add the fish and sear each side until golden brown, about 1 to 2 minutes per side. Transfer to a plate and allow to rest for a few minutes.

Assemble the plate by spooning a mixture of vegetables and tomatoes onto a serving plate. Season with salt and pepper. Top with a salmon fillet and spoon a little more oil around the outside of the dish. Drizzle balsamic vinegar around the edge into the oil. Squeeze the fresh lemon onto the salmon and garnish with the freshly chopped herbs.

no reason to do anything differently. He has been a constant support to farmers and producers, giving them an assured income in a difficult economy. But it's not enough to be local to supply Locals; you also have to be good. By offering the business cards of his suppliers, Ronald is putting them forward for the public to discover and support as well. The Locals website is a great place to start exploring island food artisans in the Comox Valley, as he lists his suppliers there as well as at his restaurant. If you eat at Locals, you see how Ronald uses the products, and you'll get some ideas there as well. People used to say the only thing they didn't like about Locals was the location, in a strip mall in downtown Courtenay. (For the record, that never bothered me!) Now Locals has relocated to a site people feel is much more appropriate to the food Ronald cooks and the excellent service his wife and front-of-house manager, Tricia, provides; they are in the Old House, a heritage building not far from the banks of the Courtenay River.

Roasted cacao beans, Organic Fair

CHOCOLATE

There are many fine chocolate makers on Vancouver Island and the Gulf Islands. Of course, chocolate is not a local ingredient, but more and more of our chocolatiers are starting to work with fair-trade cocoa, which guarantees decent working conditions and wages for the producers. You know there are two types of people in the world—cheese people and chocolate people. I am in the camp of the chocolate people. I could give up eating cheese, but never chocolate. Dark chocolate is my favourite, but I don't mind savouring well-made milk chocolate from time to time. All the health benefits recently ascribed to chocolate come from the dark variety, however. Here are some of my favourite chocolate makers in our region; most of them have distribution outside their home bases, so check their websites for retailer information.

DENMAN ISLAND CHOCOLATE—DENMAN ISLAND

It's always an adventure going over to Denman Island, but the best adventure is making your way up a twisty, wooded driveway and spotting the Denman Island Chocolate factory at the top of a hill overlooking the ocean. Daniel Terry has owned this chocolate company since he started it with his wife, Ruth, in 1998. It started as a make-work project when their plans to be market gardeners on Denman in 1994 were thwarted by an overabundance of home gardeners. Before they knew it, their high-quality chocolate bars were in great demand and the company was born. Sadly, Ruth passed away in 2004, but Daniel maintains that he and his employees continue to make their products the way she would like them to be made. The chocolate used is all fair trade, certified organic, as are the other main ingredients that go into the flavoured bars; one is Holy Molé, a Mexican-inspired bar that is spiked with organic chipotle chili powder, not an easy ingredient to source in quantity in organic form. Daniel has fun with the names of his bars, which are a bit outside the box: Rosemary, Baby is the name of his 70 percent dark chocolate imbued with a hint of fragrant rosemary, and Razzle Dazzle has dried raspberries stirred into the mix. Other than his distinctive bars with the bright foil inner wrappers poking out from their parchment-coloured labels, Denman Island Chocolate fans also look for limited run seasonal offerings, such as chocolate frogs, hearts, bunnies, Santas, and even jolly Buddhas. One percent of the company's gross income each year is donated to local conservation groups.

ORGANIC FAIR—COBBLE HILL

Marisa and Kent Goodwin of Organic Fair (www.organicfair.com) are becoming well known for many of the certified organic products manufactured or packaged at their farm in the Cowichan Valley, including soda syrups, spices and rubs, flavoured salts, and more. But what they are most proud of is their bean-to-bar chocolate, a venture they began in 2013. They import fair-trade, organic cacao beans from plantations around the world, carefully roast them, and even more carefully turn them into dark chocolate bars in a process that takes days but reflects the *terroir* of where and how the beans were grown. Their Nicaraguan bar, for example, has a distinct flavour of cinnamon to my palate (no cinnamon is added), while the chocolate they create from Madagascar beans is intensely rich and fruity. Along with their bean-to-bar products, Kent and Marisa make other bars using some unique ingredients, such as maple syrup powder, sun-dried apples, and alder-smoked salt in their Canadian bar and a heady blend of chipotle, cinnamon, cardamom, and vanilla in their Chiapas bar. They also sell certified organic baking chocolate for when you want something special to add to a dessert, like Marisa's Maple Hazelnut Chocolate Pâté (page 61).

Organic bean-to-bar chocolate from single-origin plantations around the world

ROGERS' CHOCOLATES—SIDNEY AND VICTORIA

This is really the granddaddy of all the chocolate-making businesses in British Columbia. It began over 125 years ago in the back of a grocery store in Victoria owned by Charles Rogers, who became known as "Candy" Rogers when his sweets became popular. One year, close to Christmas, I found myself in the Rogers' chocolate factory not too far from downtown Victoria. After I put on my lab coat and hairnet, I was literally a kid in a candy factory as I was shown around by Cornell Idu, the master chocolatier at Rogers'. First of all, the aroma just surrounds you and I think I was floating off the floor just from that. You can't believe what it's like to see giant slabs of chocolate and vats of melting chocolate and little nougats heading down a conveyor belt to be drenched in more chocolate! While the company has historic roots, Cornell is a very modern chocolatier and is constantly inventing new products to satisfy the cravings of chocoholics, including a line of organic chocolate bars and my latest favourite, pink and white sea salt-topped vanilla caramels. Part of Rogers's strength is that not only does it make good-tasting chocolate, but it also puts those products in wonderful packaging, often featuring local artists, for a true keepsake.

Chocolate production line at Rogers' Chocolates

YOU MIGHT ALSO WANT TO TRY:
DARK SIDE CHOCOLATES—CUMBERLAND

Worth the side trip from nearby Courtenay or Comox to try their selection of organic, fair-trade chocolate bars and truffles.

GABRIOLA GOURMET GARLIC—GABRIOLA ISLAND

Turns out that Ken Stefanson, the Gabriola Gourmet Garlic guy, is also a dab hand at making chocolate bars, truffle style or solid, some with flavours, and yes, a garlic-flavoured chocolate bar.

HOT CHOCOLATES—COURTENAY

Walk into this well-stocked shop on one of Courtenay's main streets and you may never come out again—chocolate and gelato overdose. Chocolate truffles, chocolate bark, chocolate bars, and house-made fudge, and twenty-four seasonally inspired flavours of house-made gelato and sorbet.

SALISH SEA CHOCOLATE COMPANY—SALT SPRING ISLAND

The delicious chocolate bars springing from the charming Salt Spring Chocolate Cottage are made from rich Belgian chocolate, but it's the packaging that I love most, with the Crow Bar and Bear Bar sporting artwork by renowned Haida Gwaii artist Jim Hart. A special gift box in cedar featuring the crow design and holding four chocolate bars is also available.

Marisa Goodwin's Maple Hazelnut Chocolate Pâté
Serves about 6

This can be kept in the fridge up to 5 days in advance of devouring. Please remove from fridge a minimum of 15 minutes before serving.

Prep time: 20 minutes, then chill for about 3 hours, until solid.

Special tools: You will need a 2-cup (500 mL) mini-loaf pan lined with one piece of cling film pressed into the inside of the pan, with the excess hanging over the sides, and a fine stainless-steel sieve.

3 Tbsp (45 mL) toasted, peeled hazelnuts, crushed
1 to 2 pinches of fine-grain sea salt
¾ cup (175 mL) finely chopped Organic Fair 60% cacao baking
  chocolate
2 Tbsp (30 mL) unsalted butter, at room temperature
½ cup (125 mL) minus 1 Tbsp (15 mL) whipping cream
1 Tbsp (15 mL) Cowichan Valley bigleaf maple syrup (or regular
  maple syrup)

Line the bottom of the cling film–covered loaf pan with the crushed hazelnuts and then sprinkle the sea salt over the nuts. Put your finely chopped chocolate and room-temperature butter into a mixing bowl. Heat the cream over medium heat in a small, heavy-bottomed pot until it is steaming hot and bubbles are breaking the surface. Remove from the heat and pour it through the sieve onto the chocolate-butter mixture (ganache).

Gently stir the ganache with either a spatula or spoon until just blended—don't overmix. When all the chocolate is melted (this may take a couple of minutes) and the mixture is smooth, pour it into the loaf pan and loosely cover with cling film. Chill for at least 3 hours, then flip the pan upside down onto a serving plate and gently peel away the cling film. Drizzle with maple syrup and cut into slices. Serve with fresh pears and some barely sweet whipped cream. Sublime paired with a blackberry dessert wine or Merridale's Winter Apple Cider.

Tea bushes at Teafarm; only the new growth each year is harvested to make tea leaves.

COFFEE ROASTERS
AND TEA BLENDERS

As I sit at my computer writing this, I am sipping from a special tea-brewer-and-cup combination designed with input from a teashop owner in Victoria. Inside the brewer, where you place your loose-leaf tea, I steeped a heady mixture of black Assam tea, cardamom, and vanilla bean, designed to match my Chinese zodiac sign by a tea blender near Duncan. Such is the inventiveness of just two of the tea artisans I like to frequent on Vancouver Island. Tea is my choice in the afternoon and evening, but I must start my day with coffee, and once again we are spoiled with choices. While coffee shops are ubiquitous, the people who own many of the smaller shops roast their own beans, creating signature blends according to their own philosophy of roasting. This category is highly subjective; stating which shop does the best job of roasting coffee beans or has the best blend of tea is to invite fierce debate. Everyone has their own preferences in what they want in a cup of coffee or tea. The companies listed here are those that I have tried personally and like, based on at least one of the following criteria: the quality and flavour of their products, and the service, ambience, and atmosphere of the retail outlets run by the owners. By the time you read this, more worthy companies will no doubt have been started and will eventually be added to this list. As with beer and wine, we are enjoying a renaissance of creativity in this part of the province with these products. It's easy and cheap to buy your hot or cold beverages in supermarkets, gas stations, and vending machines, but if you venture off the beaten track, your reward is unique flavour crafted in small batches by dedicated entrepreneurs.

DRUMROASTER COFFEE—COBBLE HILL

I have to admit my bias upfront here. I live within a five-minute drive of the Drumroaster, so it's my local. But I know many people who drive much, much farther to head to this café and roasting facility, and for good reason. First, the coffee. I love the espresso blend of beans and the fact that it is never roasted to the point where the beans start exuding their oil. This lighter roast cuts down on any bitterness and also means the beans I buy for my home espresso machine last longer; there's no oil on the beans that could make them go rancid. The second reason I go to the Drumroaster is for the service and baked goods. You will find me there most Saturday mornings by nine, enjoying an eight-ounce Euro-style cappuccino along with a decadent orange-coconut brioche. The service comes from the Oglend family. Father Geir and son Carsen roast the beans in the roastery and training centre next door and make sure the various coffee machines are all in good shape. Mother Pat is responsible for the brioches, along with muffins, scones, cookies, and some grilled sandwiches, and daughter Courtney is a barista extraordinaire who also educates new staff. This may be at the Drumroaster or somewhere else on the island, as the Oglends also roast coffee beans to order for many cafés and restaurants. The beans they purchase are often direct trade from the farmers, in order to ensure they get a fair price for their efforts. I almost always bump into someone I know there, which speaks to the dedicated following the Oglends have built and the quality of their products and service.

LEVEL GROUND TRADING—VICTORIA

One of the best-known companies that believes in using fair-trade coffee from small farmers is Level Ground Trading (www.levelground.com). The four families who founded the company back in 1997 have increased it into a thirty-employee-strong workforce, now occupying their third production

Caffè latte art at Drumroaster Coffee

facility, having outgrown the previous two. Stacey Toews, one of the founders, told me they see themselves as a bridge between the producer community and the consumer community. When the company changed its packaging a few years ago, it started featuring photos of the farmers consumers help support on every bag, and that's all part of telling their stories. People are still learning about what can be a shifting definition of fair trade, which can depend on which certifying agency farmers belong to. Then there is direct trade, whereby the roasters buy beans directly from the farmers without a broker in the middle. Level Ground is promoting more direct trade, while at the same time making sure their customers understand their products. In addition to the coffees, Level Ground also imports certified fair trade and organic tea, dried fruit, cane sugar, and coconut oil. Once you start snacking on the dried mango, you'll never stop!

MURCHIE'S—VICTORIA

I'm including Murchie's in this group as an island food artisan even though the company has several locations on the Lower Mainland and the head office is in Richmond. I think you can really call the Murchie's in the

Alhambra building on Government Street the flagship store. It looks as if it has been a permanent fixture in Victoria, although the 1907 building was renovated in 1986 and the ground floor became the new home to Murchie's. The company goes back to 1894 when John Murchie came from Scotland to New Westminster to found Murchie's Tea and Coffee. Now the company specializes in over a hundred different blends of fair trade teas and coffees, but the real treat is walking in the front door on the café side of the store and struggling to decide which of the array of pastries and sweets to choose from to go with your tea or coffee. I'm quite content with a pot of Earl Grey and a currant scone and clotted cream, carried to my table on a fancy metal tray. Makes me feel like I am an honorary member of the British Empire, if just for a few minutes in the afternoon (and it's much cheaper than afternoon tea at the Fairmont Empress!).

ROYSTON ROASTING COMPANY—ROYSTON

I admit it: I like shiny, bright objects. That's what drew me to Dyan Spink's table at the Comox Valley Farmers' Market a few years ago. Dyan was selling coffee beans she had roasted herself, but the photo on her table showed the bright, shiny drum-style roaster with the hand-tooled copper cladding that came all the way from Turkey. Behind the shine is Dyan's mastery of coffee roasting and her business know-how. After years of running her own businesses (including coffee-based businesses) and teaching people how to strike out on their own, Dyan and her husband, Gary, have come to roost in Royston. Their building, right on the Old Island Highway, now houses their beautiful roaster in the basement, where people come to learn about coffee and have their picture taken with the Ozturk roaster; upstairs, a full-service

Coffee ready for delivery from Level Ground Trading

Coffee roaster imported from Turkey at Royston Roasting Company

café offers their coffee products and breakfast and lunch selections as well as a frozen yogurt machine fuelled by their neighbours down the street, Tree Island Gourmet Yogurt (www.cultured-dairy.com). They also do custom roasting for a variety of other businesses and will even take your picture and put it on a bag of coffee beans. All coffees offered are fair trade organic, with more emphasis being placed on direct trade, through which more money goes to the coffee farmers instead of to a third-party certifier. Dyan is happy to have a permanent home for the Ozturk roaster. "We used to have it in the garage at our house. People would drop by on the weekends to pick up their bags of coffee and then ask us to make them a cappuccino while they were there!"

SILK ROAD TEA—VICTORIA

Daniela Cubelic founded Silk Road Tea in 1992 and since then she's been a genuine ambassador of tea to thousands of contented sippers. Whenever I speak with her, I learn new things about tea—what's in it, the health benefits, the flavour profiles, what shouldn't be in it, and so on. My favourite way to brew a loose-leaf tea just for myself is with the TipCup she helped design that is now being sold around the world

Teapot sculpted by Margit Nelleman at Teafarm

and, of course, at Silk Road. The bottom of the teacup is dual-angled. Tipped to one side, the hot water infuses the loose tea you've placed in a chamber lined with a filter. Tip it upright, and the tea stops brewing. Her enthusiasm for all things tea is mirrored in her staff, who are always ready with help or advice. Silk Road always has some sort of tea ready for you to try when you walk in the door, although there isn't always a door; sometimes you will find Daniela or some of her employees at a food festival, doling out free samples that were carefully chosen for the occasion. Look for the new Silk Road shop that opened in the Victoria Public Market in 2013.

TEAFARM—NORTH COWICHAN

When I first visited Teafarm it was called Artfarm, since many of the original products being sold there were Margit Nelleman's works of pottery. Margit and Victor Vesely moved from Vancouver to North Cowichan to live their dream of combining a farm with a gallery and tea shop. I was drawn there by Margit's teapots. They reminded me of the artistic style in the animated Beatles movie *Yellow Submarine*: elongated pour spouts, bulbous belly-like pots, whimsical tops, elaborate designs painstakingly etched by hand. As Artfarm evolved into Teafarm, Margit and Victor decided to import fairly traded teas from around the world in an effort to keep artisan tea growers in business. There are many to try when you visit their shop at the farm or stop to chat with Victor at a farmers' market, like the pine-smoked Chinese black lapsang, with its heady fragrance, or the hand-rolled little balls of jasmine tea. One favourite is their traditional Earl Grey tea that has been enhanced with lavender grown on their farm. They make other blends with homegrown mint, chamomile, stevia, stinging nettle, and calendula. They have also developed blends of teas to reflect the character of people born under Chinese zodiac signs. I'm a Dog, and I love my signature blend. If you visit the farm, be sure to have a look at the tea plantation. Victor is nurturing a few dozen plants to see how they fare in our climate. So far so good!

YOU MIGHT ALSO WANT TO TRY:
MOZIRO COFFEE—SHAWNIGAN LAKE
ORGANIC FAIR—COBBLE HILL
SALT SPRING COFFEE—GANGES AND TSAWWASSEN
STICK IN THE MUD—SOOKE
2% JAZZ—VICTORIA, TWO LOCATIONS
DISCOVERY COFFEE—VICTORIA, THREE LOCATIONS

Seth Burton of Cosmo Knives putting an edge to one of his creations

COOKING GEAR AND
KITCHEN SHOPS

Anyone who has ever visited my kitchen knows that I like good kitchen equipment: high-quality pots and pans, knives, and—gadgets. I have pretty strict guidelines when it comes to gadgets. They really have to work, and they really have to be useful. You'd be surprised how many gadgets you can buy that don't really make your life all that much easier or don't stand up at all to regular use. Before I give you a list of shops where you can find good kitchenware, I want to tell you about two specialty manufacturers we are lucky to have in this region. Their products are not for everyone, but they are true artisans in their fields.

COSMO KNIVES—SALT SPRING ISLAND
I've collected a few knives over the years—my bread knife, my filleting knife, various paring knives, a cleaver, and a bunch of knives commonly known as chef's knives, the all-purpose sort that can be used for most chores in the kitchen, from slicing to cutting to chopping. I am always on the lookout for the next great knife, one that might feel better in my hand, keep its edge longer, or slice a tomato better, so when I heard about Seth Burton's knife-manufacturing shop (www.cosmoknives.com) on Salt Spring Island, I had to go visit. Seth's Cosmo knives are made from scratch. He starts out with raw hunks of steel, heats them and presses them

A set of Cosmo knives partway through the manufacturing process

and rolls them and cuts them and grinds them and seasons them and so on until he has a finished product. His workshop is jammed with grinders and presses and a forge, much of it built or designed by Seth himself. Seth started off as a cabinetmaker, thought that was what he wanted to do, and dabbled in blacksmithing and making tools. A friend asked him to make a knife, and then he and that same friend shared a little voyage of discovery in the course of which he came across a famous knife maker in the US Southwest. He spent just an hour and a half with the man, but by the end of that time Seth knew that he needed to get into the business in a serious way and, more important, that he could make a living at it. His prices range from about two hundred dollars all the way up to eight hundred dollars, depending on the complexity of the construction. When you consider how much work goes into each piece, though, and the quality of the metal and the assembly, it's not really that much more than a factory-made knife. If you don't want to splurge on one for yourself, one of these knives (especially one in his special Damasco line) would be a great lasts-a-lifetime gift for the foodie in your life who has everything. You might find Seth's business partner selling knives at the Salt Spring Saturday

Reg Barber coffee tampers, exported to baristas around the world

Market, but the best thing to do is call and arrange for an appointment to see the full range of what he can do.

REG BARBER TAMPERS—SAANICHTON

Reg Barber was a laid-off government worker who decided to start another career running a coffee shop. As he was learning how to pull espresso shots in Seattle, he realized that the world needed a better tamper. So he went ahead and made one for himself. A tamper is a vital tool used by every barista in the world who fills a brew basket—or porta-filter, as it's called in the trade—by hand. The tamper packs the coffee so that the hot water flows slowly through all the grounds at the same rate. A lot of the tampers you see are made from a simple hunk of cast aluminum, fairly rough in nature, but Reg Barber's tampers are so beautiful I consider them works of art. "One of the coffee machine companies saw my tamper, liked it, and ordered one," he told me. "And one turned into twenty, and twenty turned into forty, and it just kept going." Reg sends tampers to some fifty different countries, and the walls of his Saanichton workshop are covered with posters and photos of him

Reg Barber in his Saanichton tamper-manufacturing facility

with world barista champions who have used his tampers in competition; they feel his products really make a difference to the final quality of the espresso. This guy is a rock star in the coffee world. The next time you're in a coffee shop, have a look around the espresso machine or ask if they use Reg Barber tampers. Chances are good they do, if they are baristas who care about the coffee they make. And if you have a home espresso machine, a good tamper is the ultimate accessory.

KITCHEN SHOPS

CAPITAL IRON—VICTORIA AND SIDNEY

When my former father-in-law welcomed me to his family, I think part of my initiation was my first trip to Capital Iron. He is a sailor and a do-it-yourselfer, and he maintained he could find anything he needed to fix his boat or his house at Capital Iron. He didn't realize I would make a beeline for the kitchen-gear section and later get lost in the barbecue department. Like the aroma of pulled pork, that part of Capital Iron draws me in again and again. It has one of the most complete selections of barbecue accessories and widest variety of barbecues that I have ever seen, certainly the best I've seen on Vancouver Island. Be sure to step outside to where the outdoor kitchen has been set up, and you'll be convinced that you need to cook outside for the whole year, which is certainly possible given our usually mild winter climate. It's not just the range of gear they have there, though; it's the knowledge contained in the barbecue sales associates, led by Mike Black, who ran that department for over fifteen years and is now the president of the company. They can help you out with whatever your barbecuing needs are, whether you are committed to propane, natural gas, charcoal, electric grills, or whatever. They stay on top of the latest trends in grilling and offer a product line that runs from reasonable to luxurious. Don't tell them, but I'm thinking of moving into the outdoor kitchen area!

COOK CULTURE—VICTORIA

Cook Culture is one of the largest kitchenware stores in Victoria and is run by Jed Grieve. Jed learned the retail business at the apron strings

YOU MIGHT ALSO WANT TO TRY:
LOVE MY KITCHEN—GANGES, SALT SPRING ISLAND
This is a small space but absolutely jam-packed with useful gadgets and gear.

of his mother, who ran the now-closed kitchen and home decor shop Muffett and Louisa in Victoria's Market Square (another shop still exists in Sidney). One of Jed's great moves in designing Cook Culture was to install a large kitchen area, which is often transformed into a classroom; there, instructors offer a wide selection of cooking classes, some hands-on, some lecture-style, but all with a lot of learning and tasting. Other strong points of this shop include its extensive selection of high-quality knives, Boos cutting boards, and Staub enamelled cast-iron cookware, as well as chef David Mincey's artisan chocolate bars imported from all over the world.

FLYING FISH—NANAIMO

I first met Flying Fish owner Glen Saunders while I was working in Prince Rupert in the late 1980s. He was working in his family's trucking business and hosting fabulous dinner parties out of a little cabin he rented at Lakelse Lake. But I soon learned about his retail savvy when he bought an old house in Terrace and renovated it into a much-needed kitchen, bed, and bath shop. Then he did the same thing in Prince Rupert with his Cow Bay Gift Galley, and then again in Nanaimo with Flying Fish. Glen found Flying Fish a great home in the historic A.R. Johnston & Co. building in the heart of downtown. You can call the mix of goods in Flying Fish eclectic if you must, but I love Glen's large wall of kitchen gadgets and the corresponding shelves full of other much-needed kitchen accessories and decor items. And if you walk into the nearby furniture section, you can find unique dining room tables and chairs as well; it's where I found my sustainable mango-wood dining table.

You Might Also Want to Try:
The Housewares Store in Mouat's Trading—Ganges, Salt Spring Island

You can get almost anything you want at the Housewares Store; I even found pellets for my specialty smoker barbecue here. This shop is part of the large Mouat's Trading building in Ganges, which includes a Home Hardware franchise. You may also want to try privately owned Home Hardwares all over the region, as they generally have a more-than-decent stock of kitchen gear, from barbecues to Paderno fry pans and more.

Muffett & Louisa—Sidney

A Sidney institution for over twenty-five years. Great selection of Emile Henry cookware and the latest in modern tableware and linens.

Paboom—Victoria

You never know what you'll find in this shop, but chances are there will be something you can use in your kitchen, like Weck jars, gorgeous resin bowls, or even soap made from beer.

Pots & Paraphernalia—Duncan

One of the largest kitchen and bath shops north of Victoria, this two-storey collection is strong on all the popular kitchen cookware, bakeware, and dinnerware brands as well as an extensive line of kitchen appliances including Saeco espresso machines and KitchenAid stand mixers and food processors.

The Tuscan Kitchen—Victoria

Mauro Schelini and his wife, Gerri, have put together a wonderful collection of Italian pottery in their European-themed shop, which nearly makes me cry when I walk in because it reminds me I don't get to Italy as often as I would like! Majolica pottery from different Italian manufacturers is the main attraction here, but the Tuscan Kitchen also retails top European brands of knives and cookware and a pantry full of imported foodstuffs like high-quality extra-virgin olive oil and dried pastas. If you're into making linguine from scratch, they will be happy to sell you a pasta machine as well.

Some of the milkers at Snap Dragon Dairy

DAIRY—CHEESE, ICE CREAM, YOGURT

British Columbia's dairy industry is in its infancy compared with the Old World, or even the province of Quebec, where cheese making has been going on for centuries. While there isn't the age-old tradition of milking cows and transforming their milk into cheese and other products here, we are catching up quickly, especially with a growing list of artisans on Vancouver Island and the Gulf Islands. Milk production is quite a high-tech operation these days. I've visited farms where cows wear microchips to identify them as they enter the milking parlour and pedometers to monitor the number of steps they take each day. Too many or too few from a cow's average can alert the farmer to a possible illness or agitation. Computers monitor the daily production levels from each cow, and bovine nutritionists create specialized diets in order to optimize production. It's a far cry from the days of milking by hand into buckets and shipping the milk in metal cans.

This thriving industry provides a local source of milk for drinking and has also spawned artisan production of high-quality cheeses and yogurts, made not just of cow's milk but of sheep's and goat's milk as well. Many of our cow's-milk producers belong to the Island Farms co-operative, which was started on Vancouver Island in 1944 but is now owned by Agropur, Canada's largest dairy co-operative. Co-op members own most of the quota, as it's called, across Canada, in accordance with regulations set by provincial milk marketing boards. Luckily, our federal government has never approved the use of growth hormones in dairy cows, as they can be quite detrimental to the long-term health of the cow. However, some cheeses produced here may have milk ingredients produced outside of Canada in other jurisdictions that do allow growth hormones, such as some of the American states. When you support small makers of artisan dairy products, who use only local milk in their creations, read the labels on those products. You will never see listed as an ingredient "modified milk products." Modified milk products from the United States, such as skim milk powder, casein, and whey protein concentrates, are allowed in Canadian food products such as cheese with no labelling of their origin. If you believe in better animal welfare as part of a sustainable lifestyle, you will avoid products that may have been produced with milk from cows injected with bovine growth hormone, or rBST. While containers of fresh Canadian milk are never supposed to be produced with rBST, avoid milk products such as cheese and yogurt that list "modified milk products" or "modified milk ingredients" on their labels.

CHEESE POINTE FARM—COWICHAN BAY

Hilary Abbott has been making cheese in the Cowichan Valley since the late 1990s. I love his blue cheeses. One is called Sacre Bleu, another is Youbou Blue, a somewhat skewed pronunciation play on the North Cowichan community of the same name. One Camembert-style cheese is called St. Clair, and the inspiration for that name actually came from Sinclair Philip, owner of Sooke Harbour House, who told Hilary that he could NOT name any cheese Camembert if it was NOT made in the part of France where Camembert is traditionally made. So Sinclair ended up with a namesake cheese of sorts, which is still proudly served on the Sooke Harbour House menu. If you want to taste Hilary's cheese, the best place to go is Cheese Pointe Farm, where you can sometimes spot Hilary, toiling over his curds and whey, through the large windows he has installed in the cheese-making facility. Hilary's wife, Patty, has stocked the farm shop with all their own cheeses and products from other local artisans. You can also find Cheese Pointe Farm products at the Little Cheese Shop on Fort Street in Victoria, owned and operated by former employee Lauren Van der Haegen. My waistline would be a couple of centimetres wider if I ate all the lunch "suggestions" that Lauren posts on the Little Cheese Shop Facebook page, enticing her Fort Street neighbours into the shop on a regular basis. Please note that Hilary and Patty are no longer associated with Hilary's Cheese in Cowichan Bay.

COLD COMFORT ICE CREAM—VICTORIA

If you've ever stopped to read the label on a commercially produced carton of ice cream, you may have put down your spoon and reached for a dictionary or perhaps the Internet to figure out what all the ingredients are. Not so with Autumn Maxwell's Cold Comfort ice cream. She makes every small batch the old-fashioned way, with organic cream, milk, eggs, and cane sugar, and even a touch of salt from Vancouver Island Salt Company. Those ingredients make for a good ice cream right there, but Autumn takes it one step further by offering unheard-of, yet alluring, combinations in a never-ending swirl of creativity. I warn you that some of her flavours may not be available at all times, or maybe ever again—it's all up to Autumn. Try these on your tongue: sour cherry and rosemary; tequila-jalapeno; rhubarb; chocolate, caramel, and cookie. She sells her concoctions in pints but also puts together fantastic combinations with baked goods acting as the bread in a sandwich. So you might get maple-syrup ice cream surrounded by walnut-vanilla meringue cookies, or graham-crumb cookies stuffed with strawberry-cheesecake ice cream. There doesn't seem to be a limit to her imagination. As this book went to press, Autumn had documented in her online journal well over two hundred different flavours. She used to offer home delivery but now is content to provide a fix of her addictive products at a half-dozen shops around Victoria and from what she calls Cold Comfort HQ, her newest manufacturing and storefront facility in the Fernwood area, just off Cook Street.

LEGATOGELATO—FANNY BAY

LegatoGelato is made of goat's milk from Snap Dragon Dairy in Fanny Bay, a place name known more for oysters than for gelato. Jaki Ayton and

Karen Fouracre own the farm and make the gelato. The goats are mostly a Swiss breed, rare in Canada, called Toggenburgs. Jaki and Karen started raising goats on their farm after Karen developed a lactose intolerance, and goat's milk doesn't create the same problems as cow's milk.

As their herd increased in size they were able to sell some of their milk to David Wood of Salt Spring Island Cheese, but eventually they decided to take the processing of their product into their own hands. They decided on gelato after some research; certainly no one else was doing it. They bought a small gelato-making machine and tested recipes until they thought they were ready. That meant they needed to have some sort of licensed pasteurizing facility, which worked perfectly into the plans of Tree Island Gourmet Yogurt, which was building a dairy-processing plant not twenty minutes down the road in Royston. Now the milk and eggs for the gelato are pasteurized there, and it is also the home of their large-scale gelato maker. My favourite flavours from LegatoGelato are the lemon and the strawberry, made from Ironwood Farm strawberries that are picked just down the highway from the goat farm. A very pleasant surprise is the wild nettle flavour, which has a beautiful tang to the aftertaste.

LITTLE QUALICUM CHEESEWORKS—PARKSVILLE

Little Qualicum Cheeseworks is another of my favourite family-owned businesses that grew out of a small idea and kept growing and growing. And it also fits in with a common theme of artisans who didn't grow up in an artisan family but had some kind of experience with an artisan product (quite often in Europe) and decided they could recreate that same kind of magic here on Vancouver Island and the Gulf Islands. In this case, Nancy and Clarke Gourlay returned to Canada in 1999 after living in Switzerland for several years with an ambition to make fine cheeses like the ones they had enjoyed in that country. Their cheese business began in 2001, and in 2004 they moved it to Morningstar Farm, built their herd of Holstein, Ayrshire, Brown Swiss, and Canadienne dairy cows, and haven't looked back. In addition to making sixteen different cheeses (Monterey Jill and their Raclette are my favourites), they have built a well-stocked farm-gate store that is open seven days a week. The farm is also home to an annual Jazz, Tea and Cheesecake festival as well as MooBerry Winery, where winemaker Phil Charlebois turns out a wide variety of fruit wines, including gooseberry and cranberry, along with the more popular fruit wines made on the island, such as blackberry, blueberry, and raspberry.

MOONSTRUCK ORGANIC CHEESE—SALT SPRING ISLAND

I've had the good fortune to be able to visit with the Graces of Moonstruck Organic Cheese a couple of times on their farm. While friends affectionately refer to the pair of cheese makers as "the girls," Julia and Susan think the girls are their cows, the stars of the show, and they're right. Moonstruck cheeses are made from the milk given by their purebred Jersey cows. There's something about Jerseys that makes them special. Actually, there are two things. First, Jersey milk is higher in butterfat and protein than milk from a Holstein cow, your typical North American high-production dairy cow. That means more cheese can be produced from each litre of milk. Second, these cows are beautiful! Not to slight the Holsteins, but there's something about the Jerseys' smooth, browny-red hides and whitish noses and bellies that makes them more endearing to me. And the Graces really look after their girls, giving them access at all times to the outdoors where they can forage on pasture and allowing the calves to be raised with their mothers in the herd. These well-looked-after and happy cows help the Graces make excellent semi-soft cheeses. I'm particularly fond of their Blossom's, Baby, and Beddis, all blue cheeses, and their ash-ripened Camembert-style is also a treat. Their cheeses are available year-round in retail shops and by special mail order, but take advantage of the fact that you can purchase cheeses at the farm in the summertime, where you can fall in love with those Jersey cows with their brown coats and soft, dark eyes.

NATURAL PASTURES CHEESE COMPANY—COURTENAY

Fine cheese comes from quality milk, and that's the secret to the award-winning cheeses from Natural Pastures. The milk tradition started three

David Wood of Salt Spring Island Cheese

generations ago with the Smith family of Beaver Meadow Farms in the Comox Valley. In 2001, Smith brothers Edgar, Phillip, and Doug saw a way to capitalize on the excellent milk they were producing by adding value to it in the form of cheese. Now, in addition to the milk from their own farm, they select milk from other carefully chosen dairy farms in the area. Not only must the milk be of excellent quality, but the farms themselves must meet sustainability standards set by Natural Pastures. Head cheese maker Paul Sutter is Swiss born and trained and started making award-winning cheeses for the Smiths as soon as he joined the company in 2002. I think part of their success is thinking outside the box a bit, as along with standard brie- and Camembert-style cheeses, they produce some unusual smoked and flavoured cheeses, such as their smoked Dutch-style Boerenkaas, and five varieties based on Verdelait, a combination of cheddar, Dutch Gouda, and Swiss raclette. My favourite is the Cracked Pepper Verdelait. There is only one milk that Natural Pastures sources outside the Comox Valley and that is the water buffalo milk from Fairburn Farm in the Cowichan Valley. This is a rare milk in Canada and it is used to make *mozzarella di bufala*, a traditional, very fresh-tasting Italian-style cheese, and you can really taste the difference between this fresh mozzarella and the more dense and rubbery industrial mozzarellas produced by large companies. It comes in two sizes: one big ball to a tub or several little balls called *bocconcini di bufala*. The larger size is excellent sliced and served with ripe sliced tomatoes, basil, and olive oil in a caprese salad while the tiny balls are great on skewers alongside grape or cherry tomatoes and basil leaves in a finger-food appetizer caprese.

Salt Spring Island Cheese—
Salt Spring Island and Victoria

David Wood brought his culinary know-how with him from Toronto and started making cheese on Salt Spring in the mid-1990s, establishing himself as a pioneer in this area in artisan cheese making. His innovative packaging of see-through soft plastic containers clearly shows the flavourings added to each chevre. Plain chevre sports colourful edible flowers, a thick layer of green basil leaves infuses another package, and then there are the whole slices of lemon, hot chili paste in the form of *sambalulek*, and decadent white truffle paste. Salt Spring Island Cheese is also known for its feta cheese, two Camembert-styles, an aged goat cheese and an aged Spanish-style sheep's-milk cheese. While you're on Salt Spring, visit the farm where the cheeses are made; you can walk around and watch people at work in the cheesery through large glass windows and eventually make your way to the retail store, which is full of not only all the cheeses made there (with samples for tasting) but also many different kinds of olives sold in bulk and other local preserves and artisan food products. In my experience, it's very difficult to get out of there without several purchases that would make a very good picnic or might just get eaten in the car as you navigate the twisty roads of Salt Spring. If you can't visit the farm, you will find Salt Spring Island cheeses at the Saturday Market in Ganges, in a large variety of retailers throughout the region and as far away as Toronto, and in their own new shop just opened in 2013 in the Victoria Public Market on Douglas Street. Over the past couple of years I've become very fond of St. Jo, the goat feta cheese made by this company, and it figures prominently as the flavour that brings together my recipe for Mussels Saganaki.

TREE ISLAND GOURMET YOGURT—COURTENAY

Scott DiGiustini and Merissa Myles decided to make yogurt as part of a whole lifestyle choice when they started their family. They had a "yogurt epiphany" on a trip to France, tasting yogurt that they had never tasted before; it was plain and simple and not industrialized like most of our yogurt in Canada. Scott says the yogurts around here are really made by just two or three companies, with milk from all over Canada, so they thought going local gave them an immediate advantage. Tree Island Gourmet Yogurt uses milk from grass-fed cows from a single farm in the Comox Valley, and they use just whole milk; nothing is taken out and nothing added in other than the bacterial cultures necessary for proper fermentation and some seasonal flavours. They built a state-of-the-art processing plant in Royston, and while the licensing and certifications seemed to take forever, the number of shops now carrying their cream-top and local honey yogurts has increased enormously. Part of the great flavour of this yogurt is the cream on top. Because they don't skim off or separate the milk when the yogurt is made, a thin layer of cream rises to the top. Competition is steep in the yogurt section, and their price is higher than your common industrial yogurts, but once you realize how pure a product it is and you taste it, you'll be hooked.

Mussels Saganaki

Serves 6

An old friend from Edmonton taught me this recipe, as she had the great fortune of spending a couple of months in Greece every winter. This recipe can be made year-round using canned tomatoes. I try to use mussels from Saltspring Island Mussels or BC Honey Mussels along with the St. Jo feta from Salt Spring Island Cheese.

1 Tbsp (15 mL) olive oil
1 medium-sized onion, chopped
3 cloves garlic, chopped
1 green or red bell pepper, cored and chopped
1 tsp (5 mL) dried oregano
1 tsp (5 mL) dried thyme
1 28-oz (796 mL) can whole tomatoes
1 cup (250 mL) dry red wine
3 lb (1.5 kg) mussels, scrubbed and de-bearded
1 cup (250 mL) feta cheese, crumbled
1 cup (250 mL) loosely packed fresh basil leaves
salt and pepper to taste

In a large, heavy-bottomed pot, heat the olive oil over medium-high, then add the onion, garlic, and bell pepper. Sauté until the onion is translucent, then add the oregano and thyme. Stir around for a bit, then add the tomatoes with their juices and the red wine. Bring to a boil and simmer for 10 minutes to let the flavours develop. Return to a boil, then throw in the mussels and cover the pot tightly. Cook for about 3 to 5 minutes, or just until the mussels have opened. Discard any mussels that haven't opened. Just before serving, stir in the feta cheese and basil leaves. Season to taste with salt and pepper. Ladle into bowls and serve with lots of crusty bread.

Happy shopper (the author's wife) at the Comox Valley Farmers' Market

FARMERS' MARKETS

In 1995, I arrived in Vancouver as the Trout Lake (East Vancouver) Farmers Market was in its first year. Great timing for me, as this fledgling market soon proved that urban farmers' markets were here to stay, and I loaded up my shopping bags every week with fresh fruits and produce trucked in from the Fraser Valley and beyond. That market enabled farmers who were struggling to show that sustainable and local foods were worth producing. Like many others, when I talked with the farmers directly I started to care more about what went into (and what didn't go into) my food, and I began to look forward to trying new varieties and bumping into new friends. When I moved to Cobble Hill in 2003, it was right in the middle of a fractious time for the farmers' markets in Duncan, my closest community for Saturday markets. I write "markets" because at the time there were two Saturday markets competing for attention in Duncan, and it was all because of friction between some factions, reminding me that eating is a political act (with apologies to Wendell Berry and Michael Pollan). Now everyone seems to be happy and there is one beautiful market in downtown Duncan, where it should be.

While those schisms were healing, more and more farmers' markets were opening all over the islands, on different days of the week, in parking lots, in fields, on downtown streets. You can't keep them straight without a program. That's why there is a website—www.bcfarmersmarket.org— run by the British Columbia Association of Farmers' Markets, to let

Sweet corn at the Comox Valley Farmers' Market

you know when and where markets take place, describe the kinds of vendors you might find there, and offer advice about becoming a vendor or even starting a market in your own community. Do I have my favourites? Sure do. Duncan, of course, once given the award of the best farmers' market in the province, although I have to declare I am biased by proximity. The Comox Valley Farmers' Market, just outside Courtenay, blessed with an abundance of farmers growing all sorts of fruits and veggies. The Moss Street Market in Victoria and, whenever I can, Salt Spring Island's Saturday Market in the heart of Ganges, where nearly 150 vendors create a festive atmosphere with food and crafts. The Downtown Victoria Farmers' Market is not on my list of farmers' markets. That's because, after the pursuit of a years-long dream, organizers have created a permanent indoor market in the old Hudson's Bay building. (See page 156.)

Farmers' markets continue to grow in popularity. PHOTO: STEPHEN HAWKINS

Farmers' markets aren't just for the summer. Some operate most of the year now, and a winter visit can still mean a healthy yield of fresh Brussels sprouts, carrots, cabbages, kale, apples, local hazelnuts, and seafood frozen at sea. That kind of winter wealth makes it a little easier to wait for the asparagus and rhubarb of spring. It also breeds awareness that you can still buy local and that crops are continuing to grow—albeit much more slowly—once the hot sunny days of summer have passed. What I love about farmers' markets as much as the food is the pleasant social interaction. Every Saturday morning I chat with my neighbours at my local markets and garner gardening tips for my own garden from my favourite farmers. I watch kids learning how carrots grow and what basil looks and tastes like, and I hang out listening to local musicians playing for a friendly crowd. This shared experience is what real communities are all about.

Braised Pork Shoulder Butt with Blueberry Sauce, Beet Salad, and Roasted Potatoes
Serves 4

I came up with this recipe to show off as many local products as possible. All the ingredients, with the exception of pepper, were produced within a few miles (or kilometres) of my home on Vancouver Island. Take the challenge; see what ingredients you can find close to home by going to local farms or your closest farmers' market. You might be surprised.

For the Pork:
1 2- to 3-lb (1 to 1.5 kg) pork shoulder butt, tied (from Quist Farms)
Vancouver Island Salt Company salt and freshly ground black pepper
1 bay leaf (from my backyard)
1 large sprig fresh rosemary (from my herb garden)
2 sprigs fresh thyme (from my herb garden)
2 cups (500 mL) Merridale House Cider or apple juice

Preheat oven to 325°F (160°C). Season the pork all over with salt and pepper and place it in a Dutch oven or heavy ovenproof pot. Add the bay leaf, rosemary, thyme, and cider; cover and roast in the oven for about 3 hours, turning the pork from time to time so all sides have a chance to get some colour. When the pork can easily be pulled apart with a fork, remove from the pot and set aside, tenting with foil to keep warm. Strain the juices into a small pot or measuring cup, then proceed with the blueberry sauce.

For the Blueberry Sauce:
¼ cup (60 mL) Valhalla Farm fruit vinegar
2 cups (500 mL) fresh or frozen blueberries (Silverside Farm)
1 Tbsp (15 mL) Babe's Honey
Vancouver Island Salt Company salt and pepper to taste

Put the pot in which you roasted the pork on your stovetop and turn heat to high. Add the vinegar and stir, scraping up any browned bits at the bottom of the pot. Then add the blueberries and the strained juice you reserved from the roast. Bring to a boil. Reduce to a simmer and add the honey. Simmer until the berries are soft and broken and the mixture has thickened to a sauce consistency. (Blueberries are high in pectin, which will aid in the thickening process.) Season to taste.

For the Beets:
3 large beets (Makaria Farm)
1 sprig fresh rosemary (from my herb garden)
1 sprig fresh thyme (from my herb garden)
1 tsp (5 mL) Babe's Honey
1 Tbsp (15 mL) Valhalla Farm fruit vinegar
Vancouver Island Salt Company salt and pepper to taste

Place the beets, rosemary, and thyme on a large piece of tin foil and fold in the edges to contain them. Put the foil on a baking sheet and roast with the pork for 2 hours, or until the beets can be easily pierced with a fork. Remove from oven and let cool. Peel the beets and cut into half-inch dice. Put the diced beets in a bowl and stir in the honey, vinegar, and salt and pepper to taste.

For the Potatoes:
2 Tbsp (30 mL) butter or duck fat (duck from Organic Fair)
4 medium potatoes (from my garden), peeled and cut into half-inch dice
Vancouver Island Salt Company salt and pepper to taste

Heat a fry pan over medium-high and add the fat and the potatoes. Stir and fry the potatoes until they are soft on the inside and browned and crispy on the outside. Season with salt and pepper.

To Assemble the Dish:
Place a mound of potatoes in the centre of each plate. Carve the pork or pull apart with a pair of forks and mound it on top of the potatoes. Spoon some beets around the potatoes and pork, then spoon some of the blueberry sauce on top of the pork. Enjoy!

Fairburn Farm water buffalo, milked to make *mozzarella di bufala*

FARMS AND FARMERS

Most of the farms in this section welcome visitors or have farm-gate or farmers'-market sales. I've always felt that it's very important to get to know the farmers in your area. They have their fingers on the pulse of what's happening with the weather and growing seasons; they often provide advice on what I should be doing or even not doing in my own garden. Without exception, they are very hard workers and usually spend seven days a week during the growing season labouring to provide you with top-quality products. Don't be surprised if you see the names of these farms popping up frequently on restaurant menus around the region; chefs know a good thing when they taste it and the direct "farm to fork" movement has been gaining momentum over the past few years.

ALDERLEA FARM—GLENORA

This is a British Columbia-certified biodynamic farm not far from Duncan in the Cowichan Valley. John and Katy Ehrlic own the farm, and it certainly fits the description of bucolic. The front yard is home to gnarly, decades-old heritage apple and plum trees that still groan with loads of fruit. Spend a few minutes walking around to the back of the farm and you'll soon discover a wonderful view, down a steep hill into a green-swathed pasture with grazing animals and extra plantings of veggies. In addition to the actual growing of vegetables, the Ehrlics now supply upwards of two hundred families with vegetables through their

John and Katy Ehrlic of Alderlea Farm
PHOTO: STEPHEN HAWKINS

community-supported agriculture program, which runs from May through December. People come once a week to pick up the share of that week's harvest that they've paid for at the beginning of the season; this helps John with the upfront costs of each year's plantings. Then there is the café at the farm, where people can have a coffee and lunches or early dinners made from farm-fresh produce. John feels strongly about having people come to the farm, especially with their children, to see how things work and is more than happy to explain the concept of biodynamic farming. Don't miss their Stinging Nettle Festival, held each spring.

DEACON VALE FARM—MAYNE ISLAND

This farm is an organic jewel, bursting with produce in the height of the season along with high-quality beef and chicken. Don and Shanti McDougall produce so many fruits and vegetables on their farm that they built a commercial kitchen to preserve what they don't sell at the farmers' market. Shanti has been known to can well over three hundred large jars of tomato sauce in one day. If you knew how long it takes me to make twelve small jars of jam, you would appreciate what kind of volume that is! They make a wide variety of products that differs from year to year, depending on what they harvest, and can get up into the ten-thousand-jars-a-year range. One of their most popular products is the tomato sauce; people travel from the Lower Mainland just to get it. Don is a professional chef as well as a farmer; he was also responsible for getting the Mayne Island Farmers' Market going when he realized the need for it. After much bureaucratic wrangling, the McDougalls managed to open a small grocery store on Fernhill Road in 2011. They sell not only their own products and Don's culinary creations but also products from many other island artisans, products that were nearly impossible for Mayne Islanders to get in the past, even though they may have been just one ferry hop away.

FAIRBURN WATER BUFFALO—DUNCAN

While Fairburn Farm in the Cowichan Valley offers city slickers a peaceful farmstay in their rambling farmhouse or small cottage, the real attraction for foodies is a chance to see Canada's first water buffalo herd grazing in the nearby pastures. This fifty-three-hectare property has been a working farm on and off since 1888, but in 2000, current owners Darrel and Anthea Archer decided to import a dairy herd of water buffalo from Denmark in order to create a product unique to North America at the time, *mozzarella di bufala*. Their journey has been difficult. The European BSE scare at the time caused the federal government to order the entire herd of eighteen slaughtered. The Archers fought the order for two years but eventually lost. Luckily, the water buffalo had done what animals do: they had procreated, and all of their offspring were allowed to survive. The herd has now been milked for several years and Natural Pastures Cheese Company in Courtenay is making both large and small (*bocconcini*) balls of mozzarella. Water buffalo meat is lower in fat and cholesterol than beef and higher in minerals. The Archers sell their male calves to Island Bison in Black Creek, where the meat is eventually for sale. I'll never forget the time I stayed at the farm and watched the entire herd of water buffalo thunder past my cabin on its way to the milking parlour. Made the earth move, and my heart as well, to see these magnificent creatures on their way to provide milk for a magnificent cheese.

Harbour House Farm manager Rob Scheres

HARBOUR HOUSE FARM—SALT SPRING ISLAND

We are very blessed with a moderate climate in this part of BC. Stuff grows. Sometimes it grows so much it obliterates anything in its path, including great gardening areas. This was the case at the Harbour House Hotel on Salt Spring Island about seven years ago. Behind the hotel was a farm, about one and a half hectares, which had fallen into disuse. Putting the farm back into production was a slow process. Farm manager Rob Scheres: "It was an old farm that was completely covered in alder and blackberry bushes. It hadn't been taken care of since the 1950s. We started cutting into it and we found old irrigation lines and other signs of the old farm. Once we got everything cleared we started working on the land." It took a few years, but now Rob and his team are growing almost everything that a restaurant needs: over a hundred different products, even quinoa! Beehives produce honey and bigleaf maple trees are tapped for syrup. The farm is now the main food supplier to the Harbour House restaurant, and it's all grown organically. Visitors are welcome daily; bring your shopping bag, as there is a farm-gate shop as well.

Roasted Spaghetti Squash with Deacon Vale Tomato Sauce

Serves 4 to 6

Here's a recipe featuring Deacon Vale's famous tomato sauce. The sauce is quite flavourful, and you can really see and taste the fresh herbs that go into it. This is a great vegetarian dish that is a good showcase for the tender strands of roasted spaghetti squash.

1 2- to 3-lb (1 to 1.5 kg) spaghetti squash
2 Tbsp (30 mL) olive oil
salt and freshly ground black pepper to taste
2 Tbsp (30 mL) coarsely chopped mixed fresh herbs (sage, thyme, and chives)
1 cup (250 mL) thinly sliced garlic scapes (substitute green onions if unavailable)
1 large jar (18 oz [500 mL]) Deacon Vale Farm tomato sauce
4 oz (100 g) fresh ricotta cheese, crumbled

Preheat oven to 400°F (200°C). Cut squash in half lengthwise and scoop out seeds and pulp. Rub flesh with olive oil, salt, and pepper. Place flesh side down onto pan and roast in the oven until tender. When cool enough to handle, use a fork to separate the strands of the flesh, running the fork from stem to blossom end of the squash, then scoop squash out with a spoon into a large bowl. Toss with the fresh herbs, garlic scapes, and salt and pepper to taste. Preheat broiler. Pour tomato sauce into a shallow ovenproof casserole dish large enough to hold the squash mixture. Top the sauce with the squash, then with the crumbled ricotta cheese. Broil until cheese browns and squash is hot. Serve with fresh bread, salad, and a crisp white wine.

ISLAND PASTURES BEEF—COMOX VALLEY AND DENMAN ISLAND

A few years ago, a group of small beef producers on Vancouver Island approached the BC Ministry of Agriculture with the idea of a co-op that would supply retailers with island-raised, grass-fed beef. The ministry went

Slow Cowboy Steak
Serves 8

Grass-fed beef can cost more than feedlot beef, but if you can get your hands on a big chuck steak, you can tenderize it during the cooking process and save money at the same time, as it isn't one of the prime cuts. This is also a chance to get out that old electric fry pan you've been meaning to donate to the thrift store. It will just thrum and bubble that steak until it is fall-apart tender. Shred the meat and serve it in tortillas with the gooey sauce. If you don't have an electric fry pan, you can certainly use a slow cooker or a large, heavy-bottomed fry pan with a tight-fitting lid.

2 Tbsp (30 mL) olive oil
1 large chuck steak, at least 3 lb (1.5 kg)
2 large yellow onions, thinly sliced
1 28-oz (796 mL) can diced tomatoes, with their juices
2 bay leaves
2 Tbsp (30 mL) unsweetened cocoa powder
1 tsp (5 mL) salt
1 tsp (5 mL) cayenne pepper
½ cup (125 mL) whisky
1 Tbsp (15 mL) red wine vinegar
1 Tbsp (15 mL) dried oregano
4 cloves garlic, peeled and smashed
1 Tbsp (15 mL) each dry mustard, cumin, and chili powder
tortillas, warmed before serving
chopped cilantro for garnish

Heat on high an electric fry pan or stovetop fry pan large enough to hold the meat in one layer. Add the olive oil and fry the steak until it is well browned on both sides. Remove from the pan and set aside. Add the onions to the pan and fry until they turn translucent, then add the canned tomatoes and all their juices, and stir in all the remaining ingredients. Bring to a boil, then reduce heat to low. Put meat back in the pan, spoon some of the sauce on top of the meat, and cover tightly, cooking at low heat for at least 3 to 4 hours. (If you are using a slow cooker, transfer the sauce to the cooker after it has boiled, then add the meat, spoon sauce over, and cook at low heat.) You want to keep the sauce just bubbling very slowly. It shouldn't dry out, but if it does, you can always add some more whisky or beer. The meat is done when it's so tender you can pull it apart with a couple of forks. Shred the meat and pile it onto warm tortillas, spooning the sauce straight from the pan onto the meat. Add the cilantro. Great dish to make ahead for when the guys come over to watch the game.

to the Country Grocer chain to see if they would be interested. They said yes, and Country Grocer stores regularly sell out of Island Pastures beef (www.countrygrocer.com/our-vancouver-island-suppliers/island-pastures-beef). Here's what people are getting when they buy this beef: the co-op ensures that all cattle are calved here on Vancouver Island (and the Gulf Islands), no growth hormones of any kind are used, and the cattle are not fed any animal proteins or rendered feed of any kind—they're vegetarians! Doug Wright of Lone Pine Farm on Denman Island is one of the ranchers. It's a larger operation, with around one hundred head of cattle. Doug has been on the farm since the 1950s; it was originally his father's. He trucks the cattle, when they are ready, on the Denman Island ferry to Gunter Brothers Meats in the Comox Valley for processing and is happy to keep the tradition of raising cattle on Denman Island going.

NANOOSE EDIBLES—NANOOSE BAY

For more than twenty-five years, the farmers at Nanoose Edibles have been tilling the soil and providing organic fruits and vegetables, not only to consumers but to a wide range of restaurants as well. Owners Barbara and Lorne Ebell welcome visitors for tours and purchases from their sheltered market gazebo. From the gazebo you can see the farm stretching out with its fruit and vegetable fields, an irrigation pond, and a nice Canadian flag waving in the wind. Having a certified organic farm means keeping track of much paperwork, making sure all of your input coming onto the farm is certified organic, making sure all your workers know what to do

Barbara Ebell of Nanoose Edibles is steadfastly devoted to providing fresh produce to local families.

when it comes to keeping that organic certification. Barbara says that for people who want to eat fresh food unadulterated by artificial pesticides or fertilizers and not genetically modified, it's absolutely necessary. "It's the only way you can be sure that you're getting a truly organic product. And I'm not going to get a young family who wants to feed their children organic food off to a bad start. Also, if it's not certified organic there are a lot more genetically modified organisms out there, and that's not the way we want to go." Barbara and Lorne have given retirement a lot more thought over the past few years. Their daughter was going to take over the farm, but she was killed in a car accident. Now they would like to turn the property into a co-operative, and there's an ongoing search for exactly the right people to take over their legacy. Perhaps some farmers will come from the many they have trained over the years and have the dedication and devotion that Barbara and Lorne have.

PEDROSA'S ASPARAGUS FARM—COWICHAN BAY

This farm has been part of my springtime Saturday-morning ritual since I moved to the Cowichan Valley over ten years ago. Coffee at the Drumroaster, then down to the farm to pick up a few kilograms of asparagus that has just come in from the field. It was formerly known as Cobble Hill Asparagus, and people still call it that, because it is the main supplier of asparagus to the Cowichan Valley and beyond for just a couple of months each year. These spears taste so good, I am usually dipping into my bag as I drive away and munching on them raw. At home, I grill them, or steam them, or chop them up and put them into risotto. If I can get a good number of slim spears, I will pickle them to use in my Bloody Caesars for the rest of the year. I seldom purchase asparagus the rest of the year; it is usually from California or Mexico and it just doesn't taste as good.

We are lucky to have this farm still operating here. As a limited-season cash crop, asparagus is extremely sensitive to weather conditions, and growing it is a very difficult way to make a living. But Jaco Pedrosa and his wife, Marlene, have injected new life into the farm since taking it over, and I'm glad to see people still flock to it for their seasonal addiction. Look for more changes at the farm over the next couple of years, such as a café and a fruit and vegetable stand where other area farmers can sell their produce.

PROVIDENCE FARM—DUNCAN

The history of Providence Farm goes back to 1864, when the Sisters of St. Ann purchased 160 hectares of land near Duncan, building first a home for young First Nations girls, then one for orphaned girls from St. Ann's Academy in Victoria. Over the years the property has served as a school for both boys and girls, but since 1979 the farm and its spectacular, metal-roofed main building have housed a great number of community services under the auspices of the Vancouver Island Providence Community Association. While therapeutic programs for those facing challenges are at the heart of Providence Farm, the production of food plays a major role. The market garden provides many kinds of produce and bedding plants that are sold at the farm store as well as at various farmers' markets in the Cowichan Valley. The commercial kitchen and dining room are now a part-time home to the Vancouver Island University culinary arts program, so students learn how to cook and serve food as part of their program. The public benefits: professional chefs-in-training make you dinner on Thursday, Friday, or Saturday nights at very attractive prices, using

Asparagus from Pedrosa's is prized up and down Vancouver Island during its short season.

as much produce as possible from gardens at the farm. The late James Barber, also known as the Urban Peasant, was a big fan of the farm, and a fundraising dinner in his name is held every year. The wood-burning oven behind the main building turns out excellent pizzas and is dedicated to his memory.

SAANICH ORGANICS—SAANICH

Saanich Organics is the joining together of three women who run farms in Saanich, along with some input from other organic or transitional organic farms in the Greater Victoria area. Robin Tunnicliffe of Feisty Field Organic Farm, Rachel Fisher of Three Oaks Farm, and Heather Stretch of Northbrook Farm are the heart and soul of Saanich Organics. They sell their products to residents through a weekly box delivery program and farmers' markets, but also to restaurants and retailers. They earn their income from over a hundred different crops, so if a few fail because of pests or weather, there are always some backups in place. Their success comes from a combination of factors, including teamwork, hard work, and developing a sense of community. But it also has to do with growing their business in a part of the world where people are becoming much more concerned about where their food comes from and how it is produced. Heather says that even given that awareness, not everyone has caught on to the idea that this is the way we should be eating: "We still import the majority of the food we eat here

Asparagus with Sage Anchovy Butter
Serves 4

I learned this recipe from chef Peter Zambri, of Zambri's in Victoria. It makes a very nice lunch or main course on its own, with the large number of asparagus spears. Cut the spears down to four per person and use smaller eggs to make it an appetizer.

1 Tbsp (15 mL) salt
32 spears of asparagus (8 pieces per person), tough stem ends
  trimmed
blanching water from the asparagus (use it to poach your eggs)
2 tsp (10 mL) white vinegar
4 eggs
4 oz (100 g) unsalted butter
1 canned anchovy per person, rinsed and chopped
4 large leaves of sage per person
freshly grated Parmigiano-Reggiano cheese

In a large fry pan, bring to a boil enough water to blanch the asparagus. Add the salt and stir to dissolve, then add the asparagus spears. Once you have blanched the asparagus for a few minutes, remove with tongs and quickly refresh them in a bowl of ice water to retain their colour, then set aside on paper towel or a tea towel to dry. Keep the asparagus water simmering below a boil and add the vinegar. (It will help the outside part of the egg white congeal more quickly.) Add the eggs to the simmering water one by one by first cracking them into a ramekin and then sliding them gently into the water. While the eggs are poaching, melt the butter and chopped anchovies together in a fry pan over medium heat. When the anchovies have melted, add the sage and gently fry until the sage leaves just start to crisp. Portion the asparagus spears onto individual plates, top with a poached egg and the sage butter, then sprinkle with some of the grated cheese. Serve immediately.

on Vancouver Island. We need more farmers like us, and we need more people to think about eating more than just the fancy heirloom tomato that gets sliced on top of their industrially produced, imported greens."

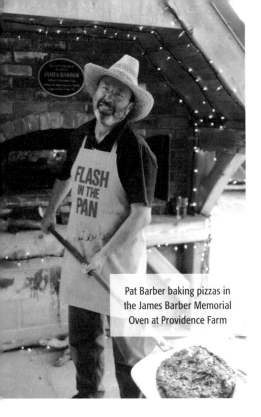
Pat Barber baking pizzas in the James Barber Memorial Oven at Providence Farm

TANNADICE FARMS—COURTENAY

For me, Tannadice Farms is all about healthy, happy pigs. Although Heather and Allen McWilliam also raise Black Angus cattle and pastured chickens, it was their pig operation that first attracted my attention when I visited their farm, and it wasn't because of a horrible smell: rather, a lack of smell. The barns where the pigs are raised are very well ventilated and the pigs have lots of clean hay to roam around in. I also didn't hear a lot of squealing or fighting. Happy, clean pigs. This is actually quite important when it comes to the finished product. Pigs that are stressed because of their living conditions or from being transported long distances to slaughter leave a number of problems in their meat. It could have a pale, unattractive colour, or poor, watery texture.

The Tannadice Farms brand is becoming more familiar to shoppers up and down the island, and grocery stores carrying Tannadice usually have cuts like chops and tenderloins, along with some country-style-cut ribs (which I love cooking long and slow on my barbecue), bacon, hocks, and even some trotters, which can be a great bargain. For a wider range of products, you are welcome to buy direct from the farm, which is open for retail sales on Saturday mornings or by appointment. Ask if you can see the pigs in their barn: there's nothing like the sight of some placid porcines to make your day.

YELLOW POINT CRANBERRIES—LADYSMITH

Most of our cranberries come from farms in BC's Lower Mainland or even the eastern United States, but there is a cranberry farm right here on Vancouver Island, busily pumping out fresh and processed cranberries.

From a distance, Yellow Point Cranberries just looks like a flat, green field. But in the fall, you can walk right into the field and see all the beautiful red berries hidden in the little bushes. Owner Grant Keefer says he and his wife started this farm because of his childhood. He grew up surrounded by cranberry farms in the Fraser River delta; when they moved to Vancouver Island, they found a piece of land that was perfect for cranberry farming, so they did what comes naturally to him. The Keefers produce about twenty different cranberry concoctions in a commercial kitchen on the farm and sell them in their cute little retail shop, the Cranberry Cottage (open seasonally). The cranberry salsa, cranberry horseradish jelly, and cranberry amaretto peach butter are all very tasty, and they even sell a little bottle filled with dried cranberries, sugar chunks, and other flavourings to which you add your own liquor, such as vodka, to make your own cranberry liqueur. The Keefers offer guided tours of the farm in September and October, all the way from an Express tour right up to the Cranberry Lover. If you can't get out to Yellow Point, the good news is that they do a few farmers' markets up- and down-island, selling fresh cranberries for Thanksgiving. Grant notes that they want to be careful with expansion. "We don't want to get too big," he says. "We just want people to be able to come out and visit the farm, learn about cranberries, and of course try some of our fabulous cranberry products."

YOU MIGHT ALSO WANT TO TRY:
FRUIT TREES AND MORE—NORTH SAANICH

If you want to grow fruit in your own backyard, Bob and Verna Duncan offer more than three hundred varieties to choose from. That includes lemon, olive, and even pomegranate trees, which can survive our temperate island climate.

THE ROOST FARM CENTRE—NORTH SAANICH

Ten acres of farmland help fuel the on-farm bakery and bistro. Even the wheat for the breads is grown and milled on the farm. Close to the airport and BC Ferries, this farm is a good way to start or finish a journey.

Golda's pestos provide quick enhancements for almost any dish.

PROCESSED FOOD
PRODUCTS

There is something about the phrase "processed food products" that doesn't sound very appetizing. Maybe it's because I have an abhorrence of some foods that don't seem very real, like "processed cheese food." So while this chapter is full of foods that have been manufactured or processed in some way, I would prefer to call them goodies, for lack of a better word. They will add to your enjoyment of food or drink. Many of them are available in some of the retail stores mentioned in the Specialty Shops section, but that availability will constantly change and grow, so it's best to check with the company to find out exactly where you can find its creations. In some cases, they may only be found at a farmers' market, but that gives you the chance to get out and meet the people involved in the companies.

When you talk to them, you may start to get a sense of all the hard work they must do. Many of these foodstuffs started as home-kitchen ventures, with daily or weekly piles of pots and pans and counters to clean up, jars to sterilize, or bags to fill and label. Many hours go into creating the names, logos, packaging containers, and labels. Don't forget social media; they need to build a website or blog, get on Facebook and Twitter, make sure all the accounts are updated! Not to mention the financial accounts, invoices, receipts, taxes. Once their baby becomes more popular, they might have to create or rent a commercial kitchen, hire employees, and so on. It all

Artisan Edibles jellies offer robust flavours featuring island fruits.

becomes a bit daunting, especially when they may have started off on their own or as a couple; then their world changes, for the good, one hopes. It means all they do is think about their creation, the next flavour, the next sale. But somehow they persevere, and a lot of the devotion comes down to the smile they get from a repeat customer, or a story of a new way their food was enjoyed. All of us eaters are part of the process; these people need our constant support. So get out there and get some goodies!

ARTISAN EDIBLES—PARKSVILLE

Maureen Drew and Judy McArthur of Artisan Edibles in Parksville were old friends on different paths in life who just happened to get together again after twenty-five years. The now-momentous meeting took place at the Filberg Festival in Comox, where they discovered, after all those years, that they had developed common interests in preserves and marketing. They started out with just four products; now they are up to a line of ten. A few jellies are made with Vancouver Island fruits and welcome exotic twists. So you have raspberry-cardamom, blueberry-lavender, champagne-rose petal, and pomegranate-hot pepper. Then they get a little more savoury with quince *mostarda*, which is a traditional Italian preparation, apple-fig-ginger chutney, and two kinds of antipasto, one with West Coast albacore tuna, the other vegetarian. They are constantly trying to track trends that may help them develop new products. Their rose petal scone mix and champagne-rose petal jelly were on the shelves to hit the florals-in-food trend spot-on, and they developed their Meyer lemon chutney even before Meyer lemons became hip. In a relatively short time, they've come a long way from the weekend they launched the business, even though it took twenty-five years to get started!

BABE'S HONEY—SAANICH

It's been a household name for honey on Vancouver Island for more than sixty years. Babe's Honey is known for being a high-quality local product as well as for its bright fluorescent-orange labels. Charlie Warren and his wife, Alison, also known as Babe, ran the company for decades, starting in 1945 with just a few hives. Eventually they had thousands of hives positioned around Vancouver Island to allow bees to produce honey from all the wonderful flowers we have around here. After Charlie and then Babe passed away, the company eventually went into receivership, and the honey supply dried up. But Babe's Honey has come back. Brandon Schwartz used to work at Babe's, and he didn't want to see all the bees, hives, and other equipment go to waste. He stepped in, with some financial help from his father, and bought the name and everything else he could afford at auction. Brandon set up shop at the Galey's Farm stand on Blenkinsop Road and started rebuilding the business, and people were glad to see those bright labels coming back. Be sure to take the

YOU MIGHT ALSO WANT TO TRY:
TUGWELL CREEK HONEY FARM AND MEADERY—SOOKE

opportunity to taste the varieties of honey sourced from different flowers, such as raspberry or blueberry; there really is a marked difference in flavour. At the Galey's Farm shop you can taste all the honeys before you buy, and the shop smells great, not only from the honey, but from all the beeswax candles available as well.

DAD'S WESTCOAST AWESOME SAUCES—LAKE COWICHAN

The name of the first hot sauce made by the Newtons of Lake Cowichan is a mouthful: Dad's Westcoast Wildfire Awesome Sauce (www.wildfiresauce.com). The Dad is Jon Newton, father to teenager Emma. Jon wanted Westcoast in the name. Wildfire comes from the heat in the sauce and from a wildfire the family witnessed from their car while discussing names. And the Awesome part of the name? Apparently, that's what teenagers say when something is really great. The Newtons got into making the sauce when the economy tanked in the late 2000s. Jon says, "I've always loved hot sauce, and when we were thinking about another way to make money, it seemed like a natural; people love to eat, they love good food, and a gourmet hot sauce that is local and different should work." Although Jon is the real hot-sauce fan, it's his wife, Liz, who developed the formula. They use fresh peppers grown in a Chemainus greenhouse, fresh ginger and garlic, no preservatives, and no artificial flavours. Since the original version of Awesome Sauce came out, Liz has developed a line of meat rubs and four other varieties of hot sauce, which vary in heat and taste. They all have a certain something I find hard to describe, but it gives them a very distinctive note on the palate. It's difficult to compete with all the other hot sauces on the market, but I believe this certain *je ne sais quoi* gives them an advantage. The sauces are now available at a growing number of retailers up and down the island, and the Newtons make regular stops at various farmers' markets.

EATMORE SPROUTS—COURTENAY

It's easy to dismiss a box of alfalfa sprouts or pea shoots as just another product you pick up at the grocery store until you see how much work goes into making sure the sprouts in the store are as safe, delicious, and nutritious as when they left the place where they were created. After touring the certified

The heat in Dad's Westcoast Awesome Sauces ranges from a mild burn to a "blow your head off" sensation. PHOTO: STEPHEN HAWKINS

organic Eatmore Sprouts (www.eatmoresprouts.com) facility in Courtenay a few years ago, I left with a new appreciation for how these delicate, tiny plants are ready for eating within just a few days of being started from seed. As she showed me around, Carmen Wakeling clearly displayed a lot of pride in the operation she and her husband, Glenn, have built since they took it over more than ten years ago. Sprouts can be contaminated with some food-borne illnesses, even when they are unsprouted seeds, so that's where Eatmore's quality control starts, and it continues all the way through

The sprouting room at Eatmore Sprouts is a marvel of constant growth.

to the packaging and shipping of their entire line, including sunflower, garlic, clover, and broccoli sprouts. It's fascinating to see all stages of the sprouts' growing process, through the staged container system Carmen and Glenn have, and even more impressive to see how they compost any waste into beautiful new growing medium for the next cycle of sprouts.

GABRIOLA GOURMET GARLIC—GABRIOLA ISLAND

Do you plant at least fifty or sixty cloves of garlic in your garden every mid-October, under the light of the full moon, buck naked? No, I didn't think so. That's why you get stuck with supermarket garlic. I grow my own garlic, but I get my garlic seed, processed garlic products, and garlic growing advice from Ken Stefanson, the owner of Gabriola Gourmet Garlic (www.gabriolagourmetgarlic.ca). I've had pretty good success following his advice, except maybe for the naked part. That's probably why my garlic is smaller than his. Ken moved to Gabriola Island in the late 1990s, and that was where he discovered garlic. He bought a small garlic business from a woman on the island who wanted to retire. That first year he did around six thousand dollars' worth of business. Now he probably does forty times that, harvesting a quarter-million bulbs of garlic every summer. Ken sells it

Liz Newton's Corn and Potato Salad

Serves 4

Liz got this recipe from her Pashtun sister-in-law and says it makes for a really nice change from the traditional Western kind of potato salad. She recommends using fresh corn kernels off the cob for a nicer crunch, but you can use frozen corn. Also, new, waxy potatoes, especially the fingerling type available at the farmers' markets, are what you need for best results.

1 lb (500 g) potatoes
3 Tbsp (45 mL) olive oil
2½ cups (625 mL) corn kernels, fresh or frozen
¼ cup (60 mL) water
3 Tbsp (45 mL) finely chopped onion
3 Tbsp (45 mL) lemon or lime juice
1½ Tbsp (22.5 mL) Awesome Sauce of your choice
2 tsp (10 mL) ground amchoor*
½ tsp (2 mL) ajwain powder*
1½ tsp (7 mL) ground roasted cumin seeds
½ tsp (2 mL) garam masala
1 tsp (5 mL) sea salt

Boil the potatoes in plenty of water until they're tender. Drain. Once they're cool enough to handle, peel and cut into small cubes. Warm oil in a medium-sized non-stick fry pan over medium-high heat and add corn. Stir for a few seconds, turn the heat to medium, and stir for another minute or so. Add the water to the pan, stir again, and wait for the water to come to a simmer. Cover the pan and turn the heat to low. Cook until the corn is just done, about 4 minutes, maybe a little less for frozen corn. If there is any liquid left in the bottom of the pan, boil it away. Empty corn into a salad bowl and add potatoes, as well as the remaining ingredients. Mix thoroughly. Enjoy right away or when the salad has cooled to room temperature. Liz likes it just as much the next day straight out of the fridge.

*Amchoor and ajwain powder can both be found at ethnic grocers. In Victoria look for them at the Indian Food Mart at the intersection of McKenzie and Quadra or at Seven Valleys on Douglas Street near Bay.

Richard Lewin of Golda's Pesto usually listens to CBC Radio One while filling his tubs of pesto.

as fresh garlic for your kitchen, seed stock for you to plant in the fall, four different kinds of pickled cloves, a cured clove with sherry and soy sauce, minced garlic, garlic chutney, powdered garlic, dehydrated garlic in plastic jars with built-in grinders, and even a couple of different kinds of garlic chocolate bars, developed in conjunction with a chocolatier he met on one of his innumerable voyages on BC Ferries. The love affair with garlic came at a great time for Ken; he had just suffered a series of four strokes and his blood pressure was sky-high. His doctor actually recommended that he eat some garlic every day to help control the blood pressure, and it really worked.

GOLDA'S PESTO—MILL BAY

Richard Lewin is pretty much the chief cook and bottle washer and pesto maker behind Golda's Pesto (www.gopesto.com). I've known Richard since before I moved to Vancouver Island, when a chef told me I had to meet Richard because he had some great stuff. So we went over to his house, where he was toiling away in his kitchen with food processors and blenders and mounds and mounds of the basil that he was using to make pesto. Richard will talk your ear off about any topic in the universe, and to watch him sell pesto at a farmers' market is a lesson in marketing and showmanship. He started with classic basil pesto and has expanded his line to include dill, cilantro, artichoke, olive, sun-dried tomato, blueberry, hempseed, and garlic scape. He also makes a spicy (a little goes a long way) skoogk, which is similar to pesto but has garlic, cilantro, and jalapeno peppers as its main ingredients. These products are very versatile and can sit in your fridge or freezer without spoiling until that very moment you really need a zap of flavour to go into whatever you're cooking. When Richard started the business, his daughter Golda was a year old, so he named the pesto after her. Eventually he had a professional kitchen built as an addition to his house, and he's traded the tiny food processor for an emulsifier that can make gallons of pesto at a time and has purchased other gadgets that make his life a lot easier, but he's still mostly a one-man show. He's been at the pesto project for over twenty years now and his little tubs of goodness can be found across the country. However, I think asking Richard if he is ready to retire is like asking a bird if it's ready to stop flying. If anything, he is getting busier and busier.

Monsoon Coast spices take you around the world, packing a punch into each small jar.

MONSOON COAST TRADING COMPANY—SALT SPRING ISLAND

The heady aroma hits you as soon as you walk through the door of this otherwise nondescript unit in a light industrial mall in Ganges. Just a few sniffs and other worlds parade through your mind—Africa, the Middle East, and a hint of Asia, all emanating from the spice-grinding, mixing, packaging, and warehouse facility of the Monsoon Coast Trading Company (www. monsooncoast.com). Ironically, Monsoon Coast owner Andrea LeBorgne says she no longer notices the heady richness in the air when she walks in the door—the price you pay for long-term exposure. But that slight dulling of her olfactory system hasn't affected her sense of flavour when it comes to maintaining the blends created by the company's founder, Doug Hall, or forging ahead with new blends since she bought the company from him. She's gone on to create a barbecue rub; although many of the original blends work quite well as rubs. Her Arabian Baharat, for example, is a splendid match with lamb chops or on skewers of chicken. Because the company is small but busy, Andrea avoids a problem common in larger spice suppliers: staleness. She roasts, grinds, and blends in small batches so that when you crack open a jar, you can smell the freshness, which makes a big difference when you are adding it to your recipes. You should also try Monsoon's Railway Chai; it really is the flavour of India in a cup.

OLIVE THE SENSES—VICTORIA

Steve and Emily Lycopolus bring an interesting perspective to this business, as part of Steve's family owns an olive grove in the Marche region of Italy, and Emily has a background in chemistry. This mix of practical knowledge and science turns out to be very important in the world of olive oil, and it was their love of olive oil that made them open this shop. They had been living in Europe for a while, enjoying good oil, and when they moved back to Canada they were disappointed in what they could find.

When you walk into Olive the Senses in the Victoria Public Market building, you don't see rows of dusty bottles of olive oil. Instead, you see shiny stainless-steel containers called *fustis*, fifteen litres in size, each with a little spigot at the bottom, each with a different kind of olive oil from a different region of the world to taste. When you taste one you like, they fill up a bottle for you and label it. Olive oil does not improve with age: it's best as soon as it's pressed. Emily and Steve rotate their oils carefully so that you will never purchase an oil older than eight months. In most cases it will be

Olive oils ready for tasting at Olive the Senses

no older than six, as they take advantage of the different harvest times in the different parts of the world. They also stock the best infused oils I've tasted. The quality comes from crushing raw ingredients, such as blood oranges, with the ripe olives before the oil is pressed. I don't use anything else for dressing my salads now. They also stock a large selection of balsamic vinegars, also available for tasting. Try the pomegranate flavour.

PASTA COMPANIES
COWICHAN PASTA COMPANY—SHAWNIGAN LAKE
KILRENNY FARM—COWICHAN BAY
PRONTISSIMA PASTA—COURTENAY

With my Italian background, I have put away a fair amount of pasta over the years—two or three times a week at home growing up. Lasagna was the special dish for family gatherings, and the funny thing is that we rarely ate fresh pasta noodles; most of it came out of a box. Now I've learned how to make fresh pasta, but most people don't take the time to do that, which is where these artisan pasta companies come in. First up is the Cowichan Pasta Company (www.cowichanpasta.com), the brainchild of a young chef named Matt Horn. Travelling through Italy and seeing so many shops selling fresh pasta convinced him that we needed that kind of choice on Vancouver Island. Matt makes both extruded pastas and stuffed ravioli, which he used to make painstakingly by hand until he managed to afford a machine. He uses only Vancouver Island ingredients, including salt from Vancouver Island Salt Company, Cowichan Valley beef, British Columbia spot prawns, and vegetables and foraged items like seaweed and chanterelle mushrooms with the seasons. Even the flour comes from Vancouver Island-grown hard wheat that is milled at True Grain Bread's mill. Matt stresses that you don't need fancy sauces to complete the experience when you're eating his pastas; you don't want to overwhelm the delicate flavour of the pasta.

For pasta and sauces, try the offerings from Kilrenny Farm, owned by Deborah and Russ Fahlman. I've been buying fruits and vegetables from the Fahlmans' organic farm and booth at the farmers' market for years now. They've had the dream of making pasta for sale for about twenty years, and finally they took the plunge: they renovated their farm-gate shop into

Squid-ink pasta at Prontissima Pasta

a commercial kitchen, bought an Italian extruder pasta machine, visited Italy once again to learn more about making pasta, and started cranking it out. I love their *malfadine*, a ribbon of pasta that is ruffled along the edges and really holds the sauce, such as Deborah's marinara sauce made from tomatoes grown on their property. Along with egg-based pastas, Deborah also makes spelt and kamut pastas, which are lighter on the gluten factor.

Sarah and Derek Walsh of Prontissima Pasta were on a sailboat when they stopped in Venice for the winter. They learned to speak Italian and make pasta. Now they have a small shop and storefront selling fresh pasta in Courtenay. That's their story in a nutshell. The whole story of how Sarah, from Quadra Island, and Derek, from Dublin, Ireland, ended up in Courtenay with a small pasta company would probably fill a book, but it did involve a decision to return to a less populous region of the world where people love food. They wanted people to be able to buy fresh pasta made with local eggs, as well as their line of pestos, with a few surprises such as Walnut, Artichoke and Roasted Garlic, Roasted Red Pepper, and Roasted Butternut Squash, the latter two types being available only strictly in season—summer for the bell pepper and winter for the squash.

Prontissima Pasta is available via their storefront in Courtenay and occasionally at the Comox Valley Farmers' Market, while you can find Cowichan Pasta at the Cedar and Moss Street (Victoria) farmers' markets and in the freezer case of retailers from Nanaimo south. Kilrenny Farm pasta can be found at the Duncan Farmer's Market, their farm-gate store, and a growing number of retailers on South Vancouver Island.

PATRICIA CHUEY'S GLUTEN-FREE BLEND—LANTZVILLE

When I heard that an island-based nutritionist had developed a gluten-free baking blend for things like cakes, cookies, and muffins, I thought she was making a good business move to take advantage of a trend. But that turned out to be not really the case. Patricia Chuey (www.patriciachuey.com) developed this blend mainly for herself. A few years ago she was finally diagnosed with celiac disease. Armed with that diagnosis she started trying various gluten-free products, and she just wasn't happy with what she found. They were low in nutrition, made mostly with white rice flour, crumbly, tasteless, and expensive. So she decided to start baking her own gluten-free goodies using her own blend, made of sorghum (a grain), white beans, tapioca, corn starch, and xanthan gum, which is made from corn sugar and helps to make dough stickier and keep things together. The sorghum and beans are sourced from the prairies. Patricia is quick to point out that she doesn't believe in people going on a gluten-free diet if they are not gluten-intolerant. But she does advocate being careful with the gluten products that you do consume; using more whole-grain foods and less-processed flours are much healthier choices. To try more recipes, you can order Patricia's cookbook, which she has revamped for gluten-free diets. *Eating for Energy Without Deprivation: The 80-20 Cookbook* (Gluten-Free Edition) is now a Kindle edition e-book.

YOU MIGHT ALSO WANT TO TRY:

If you don't like to bake, there are some tasty gluten-free products out there. Chef Janice Mansfield supplies gluten-free goodies to these Victoria spots: Nourish, AJ's Organic Cafe, Township Coffee, and the Tin Roof in Cook Street Village. For more info: realfoodmadeeasy.ca.

SALTSPRING SUNRISE PREMIUM EDIBLES—SALT SPRING ISLAND

Olive oils from all over the world are a staple in my kitchen, but when I want to use a nut oil in my baking, salads, or frying, I have a local alternative: certified organic BC hazelnut or walnut oil, expeller cold-pressed on Salt Spring Island, from Saltspring Sunrise Premium Edibles (www.saltspringsunrise.ca). This is another great story about someone getting interested in where their food comes from and discovering that something they wanted wasn't available here but the potential for producing it was. Company owner Bejay Mills: "The harder I looked, the more I realized that nobody around here was making oils, and they certainly weren't making hazelnut oil. So I got an expeller and we set it up on my parents' farm on Salt Spring and we started pressing some hazelnut oil." He'd never done anything like this before, but Bejay does have experience in the agricultural field; he works as an entomologist on the Saanich Peninsula, studying and developing natural, biological methods of controlling pests in our crops. So that was why producing a certified organic oil was a priority for him. Because he couldn't find enough organic hazelnuts on Salt Spring, some of them are sourced from the Fraser Valley, but he's trying to set up a co-op of farmers to grow organic nuts for him. Along with producing hazelnut and walnut oils, Bejay is selling hazelnut flour, a product made from the nutmeal left over once you've pressed the oil out. It is gluten-free. His research also continues into growing a special variety of pumpkin known for the oil that comes from the seeds, and he has been talking with local farmers about pressing certified organic canola seeds into oil, as well as local organic black oil sunflower seeds.

SEA SALT
VANCOUVER ISLAND SALT COMPANY—COBBLE HILL
CLEVER CROW HERBS, SPICES AND SEA SALT—COURTENAY
SALTWEST NATURALS—OTTER POINT

This may sound hard to believe, but I once got very excited watching water boil. The charge came from watching our first artisan sea salt manufacturer, Andrew Shepherd, of the Vancouver Island Salt Company (www.visaltco.com). As I walked up his driveway, I took in the aroma of a wood fire and

Summertime Pasta from Prontissima Pasta
Serves 4

With so many great fresh ingredients available from farms in the Comox Valley, Sarah Walsh had no problem coming up with a way to use them with their fresh pasta and one of their pesto sauces as well.

½ cup (125 mL) finely chopped red onion
4 cloves garlic, crushed
2 Tbsp (30 mL) olive oil
1 cup (250 mL) fresh peas
½ bunch of asparagus, chopped into bite-sized chunks
1 large (8 oz [200 g]) container Prontissima Arugula or Basil Pesto
1 large bag (1 lb [500 g]) Prontissima Traditional Egg Tripolini
12 cherry or grape tomatoes, halved or quartered
½ cup (125 mL) freshly grated Parmigiano-Reggiano cheese
a few fresh basil leaves and more Parmigiano-Reggiano cheese
    for garnish
freshly ground black pepper

Put a large pot of salted water on to boil. In a large fry pan over medium heat, sauté the onion and garlic in the olive oil until soft, then add the peas and asparagus. Pour in a couple of tablespoons of water and then cover the pan to let the peas and asparagus lightly steam (you want them to still have a bit of crispness to them). Have your pesto out at room temperature and ready to add. Once the water is boiling, toss in the fresh pasta and cook for 2 to 3 minutes. In the meantime, turn the heat down on the veggies and toss in the fresh chopped tomatoes. Once the tomatoes are warm and the veggies are done to your liking, take them off the heat. Drain your pasta and put it back in the pot, off the burner, with a little olive oil so it doesn't stick. Toss in the summer veggies, the pesto, and the cheese and stir until everything is coated and evenly distributed. Garnish with a nice sprig of fresh basil, more cheese, and some freshly ground black pepper. You can enjoy this on its own or with some thin strips of barbecued chicken or some fresh prawns! A very easy and healthy dinner.

Delicate crystals are the trademark of Vancouver Island Salt Company sea salt.

simmering pots of ocean water, and there was Andrew stoking the fire, evaporating the salt water until there was nothing left but beautiful salt crystals. Why salt? As a trained chef, Andrew couldn't see the sense in using imported sea salt in his cooking when we are surrounded by salt water here on Vancouver Island. So he started experimenting, at first boiling down a ten-litre bucket of water. Friends loved it, so he started using large stockpots over open wood fires to make more. Now he uses large cauldrons fired with recycled vegetable oil. His line of salts includes a *fleur de sel*, the finest salt crystals of the process, and a line of infusions ranging from banana pepper to blue cheese. "Salty Andy," as he's known, has also opened a salt and spice shop called Island Spice Trade in the Victoria Public Market in the Hudson building. His success has spawned other artisans.

In Courtenay, Lia and Brian McCormick operate Clever Crow Herbs, Spices and Sea Salt (www.facebook.com/CleverCrowHerbsSeaSalts). Once again it came down to trying to fill a void; no one in the area was making sea salt, and they worked at it steadily for six months to get the process and the texture of the salt just right. When they had nailed down their base, they started to get creative with infusing the salt with different flavours, including citrus, rosemary, and seaweed. They also make a rich red-wine infusion, the wine produced from local grapes at nearby Beaufort Vineyard

SaltSpring Kitchen Company preserves PHOTO: MELINDA DIVERS

and Estate Winery. And they sell cute little metal boxes that slide open for their salt. They are the perfect size to take on a picnic or even slip into your pocket or purse if you are the kind of salt fanatic who likes to take a little bit of the ocean with you wherever you go.

To complete the geographical spread of middle, up-island, and south island salt producers, Jessica and Jeff Abel founded Saltwest Naturals (www.saltwest.com) in Otter Point, just outside Sooke. They go out in Jeff's boat to collect water, and do not use any additives or chemicals in their infusions. I particularly like their maplewood-smoked sea salt, which also has a touch of maple sugar in it. You can't get much more Canadian than that!

SALTSPRING KITCHEN COMPANY—SALT SPRING ISLAND

When you visit the Saturday Market in Ganges, it's not hard to find half a dozen vendors who are jam, jelly, and marmalade makers. Melanie Mulherin of the SaltSpring Kitchen Company (www.saltspringkitchenco.wordpress.com) intrigued me with some of her novel creations, such as Pink Grapefruit and Rhubarb Jam-A-Lade, and Meyer Lemon and Lavender Marmalade.

"I develop recipes that are unique, putting things together that you normally wouldn't think of, like the pink grapefruit and rhubarb. I also try to make sure that many of my flavours will go perfectly with cheese, since we have so many great cheeses that are made here on the island." When I buy preserves rather than make them myself, I want something different. Melanie's creativity stands out in her blending of unexpected flavours and her attractive packaging. Top sellers include tomato jam, the pink grapefruit and rhubarb jam-a-lade, and her candied jalapenos. I nearly ate the whole jar I bought from Melanie in one sitting.

SOYA NOVA TOFU COMPANY—SALT SPRING ISLAND

Making tofu at Soya Nova Tofu Company

Soya Nova is a collection of small buildings that houses not only owner Debbie Lauzon's home but also the commercial kitchen where the tofu is made and a room dedicated to creating her dynamite smoked tofu. Debbie started making tofu when she was living on Mayne Island thirty years ago, when as a vegetarian you couldn't just go down to the corner store and buy tofu. She had learned a bit about tofu in California. She was definitely a flower child back then, but her father called her a "blooming idiot." Her big break came when her mother gave her three hundred dollars to buy a Vitamix blender so she could grind soybeans more efficiently. That grinder is long gone but the business is still thriving. She uses up to fifteen tons of soybeans every year, and she's trying to persuade some local farmers to grow organic soybeans for her. When she started the business it was called Supernatural Tofu. But that was just when good old Bill Vander Zalm was pumping Super, Natural BC, and she didn't want any political affiliations between her tofu and the BC government of the day. So she changed it to Soya Nova, Nova being her daughter's name. That's soy nice, isn't it?

Farmed Vancouver Island scallops

SEAFOOD, FRESH AND PROCESSED

If one were asked to define West Coast cuisine, no doubt fish and shellfish would make their way into the resulting description. It's no wonder: we have some of the finest seafood available anywhere in the world. Entire cookbooks have been written about our Pacific salmon and Dungeness crab. Oh, the crab! I had never bought and cooked a live Dungeness crab until I ended up in the parking lot of a nondescript hotel in Prince Rupert in the mid-1980s. In the back of his beat-up pickup truck, a crabber had a large tote bin full of just-landed crabs. "Five bucks," he said and handed me a plastic bag that seemed alive with activity from any number of points along the bottom seam. After a brief struggle to avoid getting my fingers pinched, I popped the crab into a pot of salty, boiling water. About half an hour later I was surrounded by empty shell, my fingers sticky from crab juices and melted butter. Since I learned how it worked, Dungeness crab has been part of my diet for over twenty-five years. Salmon? I've had the distinct pleasure (and exhaustion) of landing a few chinook fighters in the twenty- to thirty-pound range, later eaten as boneless fillets and carefully cured lox. I've devoured countless chunks of sockeye in sashimi and was educated in the mild yet underrated flavour of a pink salmon that had been treated with kid gloves by a sustainable-minded fisherman who barbecued it right on the deck of his boat. We

Some of our best: farmed mussels and clams, wild sockeye salmon PHOTOS: BETTINA HARVEY

also can enjoy the most delicate flaky halibut, succulent sablefish, and terrific albacore tuna.

Shellfish are the best in the world here. Tiny Kusshi oysters slurped raw from the shell, or giant beach oysters, breaded and fried; Manila or savoury clams for my *linguine con vongole*; the biggest and juiciest mussels. I won't eat shrimp or prawns that are not from BC waters. My favourites are spot prawns, but sidestripe and humpback (also known as king) shrimp are just as delicious. I even like some of the lesser-known delights, like geoduck, gooseneck barnacles, oolichan, and sea urchin. My only regrets are that some of our finest seafood gets exported overseas immediately, before we ever get a chance to enjoy it, and that a number of man-made factors are contributing to a decline in some species' populations and a destruction of fish habitat. Look for the Ocean Wise logo or those of other sustainable seafood programs on restaurant menus and supermarket and fish-shop counters. That way, you can be sure that the products you are buying are from sustainable sources. The following producers and fishmongers are the best sources I've discovered for purchasing fresh, frozen, and processed seafood in our region.

FISHMONGERS

I wish I had more fishmonger's shops to write about. They are one of those specialty shops that fell by the wayside when we started going to supermarkets, and because we don't eat as much fish as we should, perhaps, the resurgence in this kind of shop has lagged behind that of butcher shops, for example. I find that even supermarkets that have dedicated department space to fresh seafood and live tanks with crabs, clams, and mussels have woefully undereducated staff when it comes to providing information consumers want to know: whether the fish is farmed or wild, where it was caught, when it was caught, and how to cook it. That's why the following shops, staffed by either their owners or knowledgeable workers, have made it onto this list.

COWICHAN BAY SEAFOOD—COWICHAN BAY AND VICTORIA

When Anne and Gregg Best took over the struggling fish shop in Cowichan Bay a few years ago, I couldn't have been happier. With over thirty years' experience on the ocean, who better than they to supply and operate a seafood shop? They pretty much ripped out everything that had been in the shop before and installed live tanks for Dungeness crabs, clams, mussels, and oysters, as well as a set of freezers; you can pick up products that are carefully frozen so you can enjoy them all year long, without any loss of flavour or quality. There is also a wide-ranging pantry featuring products from other local artisans, cookbooks, and a selection of oils and vinegars. Gregg really didn't like to see so many of our best spot prawns heading straight overseas before islanders had a chance to taste them, so he organized the Cowichan Bay Spot Prawn Festival, which has grown bigger and better each year, raising awareness of a fantastic, sustainable seafood. In 2013 the Bests decided to make more of an impact in Victoria as well, staging another spot prawn festival there and leasing one of the largest spaces available in the new Victoria Public Market. They carry only sustainable seafood caught in BC waters or farmed shellfish approved by the Ocean Wise conservation program.

MAD DOG CRABS—DUNCAN

I first met Scott and Katie Mahon at the downtown Duncan Farmer's Market when it used to be in the train station parking lot every Saturday morning. Scott was a commercial fisherman who would bring a big cooler full of crabs to their Mad Dog Crabs stall with one or two lonely crabs burbling away in an aquarium for show. Every now and then, along with

Gregg Best (l) and Michael Abbott weighing spot prawns for Cowichan Bay Seafood during the annual Cow Bay Spot Prawn Festival PHOTO: STEPHEN HAWKINS my crab, he would try to sell me a big chunk of octopus that he had had to wrestle off one of his crab traps. The "crab shack" became so popular that Scott stopped fishing and he and Katie opened up a stand-alone seafood shop not far from downtown on Canada Avenue and now sell fish and

Voodoo BC Spot Prawns
Serves 2 or 4

I adapted this from a shrimp recipe I picked up during a visit to New Orleans the year after Hurricane Katrina devastated that city. The flavours are like the city: a rich stew of different influences, in this case, Cajun, Thai, and Italian. This recipe is great as an appetizer for four people or serves two as a main-course entrée, either on rice or with lots of crusty bread to mop up the juices.

¼ cup (60 mL) olive oil
1 Tbsp (15 mL) Cajun spice rub or other hot spice mixture
1 lb (500 g) BC spot prawns, shelled and deveined if necessary
¼ cup (60 mL) butter
2 cloves garlic, chopped
2 medium tomatoes, seeded and diced
½ cup (125 mL) Southern Comfort liqueur
½ cup (125 mL) sweet Thai chili sauce (available at most Asian markets)
¼ cup (60 mL) fresh basil leaves, chopped

Pour the olive oil and the Cajun spice over the prawns and toss to blend well. Set aside for up to half an hour. In a heavy skillet over medium-high heat, melt the butter, then add the garlic. Sauté until translucent, then add the tomatoes and stir. When the tomatoes soften, add the shrimp mixture and cook the shrimp, stirring, until they just turn opaque. Pour in the Southern Comfort, and if you're cooking on a gas stove, tilt the pan slightly into the flame to ignite it and flambé the shrimp. On an electric stove, you can carefully ignite the Southern Comfort with a long match. When the flames burn out, add the Thai chili sauce and the basil leaves. Stir again to mix well and serve immediately.

crabs caught by his fisher colleagues. They kept that name, Mad Dog Crabs, and have also opened a smaller shop, south of Duncan by the Old Farm Market, called the Shack, open seven days a week.

FINEST AT SEA—VICTORIA

Bob Fraumeni, the founder of Finest At Sea, bought his first fishing boat in 1977 and hasn't looked back, expanding the fleet and opening a retail shop in Victoria, with more locations now set up in Vancouver. The first name of Bob's company, in 1984, was Frozen At Sea Seafood Producers, or FAS. He knew back then the importance of being able to deliver a quality product, whether it was fresh or frozen. Fish caught far from port may languish for days, or even more than a week, in the hold of a boat, its freshness and firm texture deteriorating by the minute. With the freezers Bob's fleet now has on board, fish are in a -60°F freezer as soon as possible after being caught. Bob is a passionate guy. I asked him to speak at a food-culture class I was teaching at the University of Victoria, and for a short presentation, he insisted on bringing toaster ovens to heat up some smoked sablefish for the class, showed a video of the wild sea conditions he and his crew endure to catch that sablefish, and struggled to keep his temper under control while he listened to a spokesperson from the farmed-salmon industry give his spiel to my students. Fortunately, the only fuse blown was the one attached to a toaster oven, and I knew I had met someone who cares deeply about providing a quality wild, sustainable product to his customers.

NATURAL GIFT SEAFOODS—NANOOSE BAY

Albacore tuna is one of my favourite West Coast fish, and the way we purchase it makes it very easy to use. Ian Bryce of Natural Gift Seafoods (www.naturalgiftseafoods.com) has fished all kinds of species in a career on the ocean that has lasted over forty years. He still does some salmon trolling, but albacore tuna is a more lucrative fishery these days, and most of his product is shipped off to Japan. Ian was always getting requests from people he knew for tuna, so he would bring home some whole tuna. Then he decided to see how it would taste canned, so he had some done up, liked it, and started to

Luscious smoked albacore tuna lox from Natural Gift Seafoods

sell that. Soon he had got into smoked loins, frozen whole loins, and smoked, canned tuna. I love his tuna lox, which is lightly smoked and thinly sliced. My favourite, though, is his tuna candy, modelled after salmon candy with his own adaptation of that classic recipe; he uses Vancouver Island honey as a sweetener. Natural Gift Seafoods albacore tuna is certified sustainable by both the Ocean Wise and Seafood Watch programs, and the company has certification from the Marine Stewardship Council. And albacore tuna is loaded with healthy omega-3 fatty acids. What more could you want in a food?

St. Jean's Cannery—Nanaimo

St. Jean's has been serving commercial and sport fishers since 1961. The company started off very small, in the kitchen of Armand St. Jean, who

---

You Might Also Want to Try:
Estevan Tuna—Courtenay

This is another family-run fishing company. They're not from Estevan, Saskatchewan—*Estevan* is the name of their boat. They also sell tuna loins, canned tuna in natural olive oil, and smoked varieties. Look for their bright red-and-green retro-style labels on store shelves.

Top: World's largest salmon can at St. Jean's Cannery
Bottom: Just some of the thousands of cans waiting to be labelled at St. Jean's

practised smoking oysters in the kitchen, ruining his wife's plants and smearing her typewriter ink on the homemade labels. Then he stuck those labels on the plastic bags full of oysters that he would sell in local bars. Now they employ just over a hundred people in Nanaimo. Custom smoking of seafood is still a mainstay of the operation; many of the sport-fishing lodges up and down Vancouver Island send the catches of their clients to St. Jean's to be turned into lox, hot-smoked salmon, or canned salmon. Armand's son Gerard is now the company president, and he told me he credits their small size and family roots as the reasons behind their longevity. Gerard's brother plays a large role in the mechanical operations of the plant, with other family members pitching in as well. They ship seafood all over the world and pack and smoke for large and small fishing companies alike. They offer some eighty different products in all, including clam chowder, antipastos, pâtés, even canned wild chanterelle mushrooms. When St. Jean's celebrated its fiftieth anniversary, a new Nanaimo landmark was unveiled at the cannery: the world's largest salmon can, which doubles as a conference room and museum. Gerard says the idea came while the management team was crammed into his office planning the anniversary event: "We joked that we needed more room to meet, and then we got the idea that we should just build a big can right out there in the parking lot!" Don't forget to have your picture taken beside the big can when you visit the cannery; it makes for one of those iconic Vancouver Island photos.

SATELLITE FISH MARKET—SIDNEY

The Satellite Fish Market has been sitting perched over the ocean on the pier at the end of Beacon Avenue in Sidney for over fifty years, and when you walk in you are somewhat transported back in time. The only nod to modern times is the price of the fish, being advertised according to both Imperial and metric weights. This is very much a working fish-cleaning and -filleting facility, and you can watch fish being prepared for sale, as the work area is wide open for viewing. You can tell the fish is fresh because the only odour noticeable is the salty brine of the sea. The prices and types of fish are still on hand-lettered signs protected in plastic that shines just like the skin on the ling cod, snapper, and halibut.

Sidney's Satellite Fish Market beckons to those seeking fresh seafood.

There is a large poster on the wall behind the main counter—surely it's been hanging there for decades—which details the nutritive values of fish products, with the amount of fat, protein, calories, and different minerals and an explanation of what each mineral is good for. It includes nicotinic acid, which "Prevents or Cures Pellagra"* and sums everything up with this heartfelt enjoinder: FOR YOUR OWN SAKE—EAT MORE FISH. It doesn't matter that this shop is a blast from the past; the products are as fresh as they come, straight off the boat.

*Nicotinic acid is an archaic term for niacin or vitamin B_3. Pellagra is a potentially serious disease resulting from a deficiency of niacin.

SEACHANGE SEAFOODS—SALT SPRING ISLAND

A can of salmon isn't always the first thing you think of when you're con-templating the perfect gift. But delicately smoked salmon preserved in a shiny gold pouch, then packaged in a beautiful cedar box silkscreened with a north coast First Nations design? That packaging has taken SeaChange Seafoods beyond its home base of Ganges on Salt Spring Island and all

SeaChange Seafoods uses a bold First Nations design on its packaging.

the way into outer space. At SeaChange they take sustainably caught BC sockeye and pink salmon and have it smoked and canned in gold foil packages, which preserves the flavour of the salmon and also makes it very shelf-stable. It can be stored for years or shipped anywhere in the world without refrigeration. The company has developed other products, such as salmon jerky and smoked salmon pâté, as well as pâtés of crab and lobster. Then there's the outer-space connection. Company owner Anne Millerd says, "We've actually been approached by NASA three separate times over the years to supply some of our products to the International Space Station. Astronauts need treats, after all, and Canadian astronaut Robert Thirsk was the first to ask to have our products aboard, and then an American astronaut put in a request, almost like a takeout call, to see if she could get some of the same salmon she'd enjoyed on her mission a couple of years previously." Anne told me the inspiration for the name of the company came from William Shakespeare's play *The Tempest*. "Sea change means a profound transformation, and I think that's what we do with delicious salmon: change it so that it remains delicious but can be enjoyed by everyone, a great gift from Canada."

Crispy Dogfish Fillets, Mushy Peas, and Chunky Tartar Sauce
by Chef Dan Hayes, London Chef Cooking School and Café, Victoria
Serves 6

You can ask the people behind the counter at the Satellite Fish Company in Sidney if they have any dogfish fillets. Dogfish fillets are commonly used in the United Kingdom to make the national dish of fish and chips. This recipe shows how delicious this generally unwanted species can be. If you can't find dogfish, try cod or snapper fillets. Make the mushy peas and tartar sauce first, so you can serve the fish fillets hot and crispy.

For the Peas:
½ cup (125 mL) unsalted butter, divided
½ cup (125 mL) chopped white onion
sea salt to taste
3 cups (750 mL) peas, fresh or frozen
1 cup (250 mL) chicken stock
2 mint sprigs

Over low heat in a medium-sized pot, melt half the butter and fry the chopped onion until translucent but not browned. Season with salt and then add the peas, chicken stock, and mint sprigs. Bring to a slight simmer, and cook until peas are tender. Drain, reserving half the liquid in a separate bowl. Remove the mint and chop. Add to the peas along with the other half of the butter. Blend in a food processor, adding the reserved liquid if necessary, until smooth. Serve either warm or at room temperature.

For the Tartar Sauce:
3 egg yolks
1 tsp (5 mL) Dijon mustard
2 tsp (10 mL) white wine vinegar
2 cups (500 mL) vegetable oil
2 Tbsp (30 mL) diced shallots
2 Tbsp (30 mL) rinsed and chopped capers
    2 Tbsp (30 mL) diced baby dill pickles

In a large, round-bottomed bowl place the egg yolks, mustard, and vinegar. Using a whisk, combine these ingredients well; then begin whisking harder and drip in the oil a few drops at a time—you are now making mayonnaise. Keep dripping and whisking until the mixture emulsifies and thickens. (You can also do this with a hand blender or in a food processor, but keep adding the oil a few drops at a time.) Add the diced shallots, capers, and pickles, mix well, and refrigerate until ready to use.

For the Fish:
fillets from 1 medium or 2 small skinned dogfish
½ cup (125 mL) all-purpose flour
2 eggs, beaten with a splash of milk
2 cups (500 mL) *panko* bread crumbs
canola oil for shallow frying
flaked sea salt
freshly ground black pepper

Cut the fillets of dogfish into bite-sized pieces (fish finger size) and dredge first in flour, then egg, and then *panko* bread crumbs, pressing the crumb firmly onto the fish to coat it.

Fry until golden brown in small batches in hot canola oil. Drain on paper towel, then season heavily with sea salt and a pinch of black pepper. Serve with your tartar sauce and pea purée.

YOU MIGHT ALSO WANT TO TRY:
PORTUGUESE JOE'S FISH MARKET—COURTENAY

Portuguese Joe's might look like something that washed up on shore during a high tide, but this seafood shop, on the seaside road between Courtenay and Comox, has been a family-run business for more than forty years, named after the late Joe Veloso, a Portuguese immigrant. You'll find most West Coast seafood catches here, and it's also a great place for birdwatching, as gulls and other scavengers hang out in anticipation of a daily feed of scraps from the shop.

Fresh, raw oysters from Baynes Sound are ranked among the best on the coast.

It's a place to buy fresh and frozen seafood in Tofino, but it's also where I have had my Clayoquot Sound salmon catches sent for filleting, smoking, freezing, and delivery to my door in excellent condition.

BC SHELLFISH

I could write a whole book just about the BC shellfish industry. Its roots are ancient. We have the proof of this in middens, the archaeological name for trash heaps made up of millions of empty shells discarded by our First Nations who lived near the coast and took advantage of the vast bounty of the sea within steps of their front doors. Our commercially available shellfish is now farmed in an industry considered sustainable by the current certifying agencies.

Oysters: I'm not sure who the first brave soul was who pried open an oyster and devoured what he or she found inside, but that person led the way for generations afterward to enjoy a taste of the ocean that is both nutritious and hunger-satisfying. Our oyster farmers on the west coast produce a high-quality oyster, because we have clean ocean waters that are chock full of nutrients that oysters love to gobble up. They are filter feeders and can filter over a hundred litres of water in a day. They are high in protein and very nutritious because of the zinc and other minerals and vitamins they contain. An oyster ready for market is greatly influenced by its grower. Although the oysters are all the same species, the flavour, shape of the shell, and hardness of the shell are components the farmer can influence through his or her techniques. Some oysters spend all their time in shallow water on the beach. Others are grown at greater depths in colder water, affecting growth rates and shell development. Some oysters are removed from the water and tumbled in a machine to remove the wispy edges of shell, which ends up changing the meat-to-shell ratio. Some oysters may be tumbled a few times, others up to twenty-five times in their life cycle. All this means that you will never get bored with tasting oysters produced here since they all have such different flavour profiles. No fewer than four federal government agencies work with the oyster farmers to ensure the safety of the product for consumers, as well as the quality of the habitat where the oysters are raised. Some of my favourite oyster producers in our region include:

FANNY BAY OYSTERS—UNION BAY

One of the largest producers on Vancouver Island, this company exports its oysters and other shellfish products around the world. You'll find them in many retail outlets and restaurants, but the company also operates a small retail shop near the Buckley Bay ferry terminal, from which you leave for Denman and Hornby Islands.

THE OYSTER MAN—CORTES ISLAND

I have to include Brent Petkau, the Oyster Man (www.theoysterman. com), in this list even though it has become a lot more difficult to get his oysters in this region. For a while, the jovial, bewhiskered Brent could be found all over the place in his Che Guevara-style beret and Join the Oyster Revolution T-shirt, shucking his top-quality, beach-finished Royal Courtesans at special events and selling upwards of a hundred thousand oysters a year to restaurants. But Brent says restaurants wouldn't pay the price he needed to make any profit, so he loaded up his truck with oysters and moved to—Nelson. Part of the move was a family decision, so his kids could have better access to schools, but he also decided to sell his oysters directly to the public instead of through a middleman. Brent travels back and forth between Nelson and his oyster farm on Cortes Island, bringing loads of organic apricots to Cortes residents in season and stopping here and there on his way back to Nelson to drop off batches of oysters to his regular customers. Then there are the oyster nights at BiBO restaurant in Nelson and the "Oyster Oasis," a particular parking lot in Nelson where he dispenses oysters to the waiting masses from his truck. He will still pop up from time to time at events such as the Harvest Grape Stomp (and oyster slurp) at Salt Spring Vineyards every October. If you can't find Brent and his raw Royal Courtesans, you can still enjoy his most excellent smoked oysters by mail order, shipping included, anywhere in Canada.

These smoked oysters from the Oyster Man are moist nuggets of flavour.

Keith Reid of Stellar Bay Shellfish is an innovator in the aquaculture industry.

PENTLATCH SEAFOODS—COURTENAY

Pentlatch Seafoods (www.komogway.com) is owned by the K'ómoks Nation and produces a variety of oysters from locations around Baynes Sound, Vancouver Island and the Gulf Islands' primary shellfish-producing area. Pentlatch is the name of one of the traditional houses of the K'ómoks Nation, and their flagship oyster is the Komo Gway, named after the Ruler of the Undersea.

STELLAR BAY SHELLFISH—BOWSER

I spent a few hours with Stellar Bay (www.stellarbay.ca) oyster farmer Keith Reid one day and learned more than a few things about growing oysters, while witnessing the ingenuity required to make a living as a shellfish producer. Keith isn't just a farmer; he's an inventor, a marketer, a jack-of-all-trades who realized you can't sit still in the shellfish industry. Much of the equipment necessary to raise oysters successfully is custom-designed by Keith, and he also realized that having a well-branded type of oyster was important to his sales. That oyster is the Kusshi, a small oyster with a deep cup and strong shell. Its small size and sweet flavour makes it the ideal entry-level oyster for people nervous about swallowing raw shellfish. Stellar Bay shellfish are only available at restaurants and from wholesale distributors and higher-end seafood shops.

Clams: Nearly all of the oyster growers on the West Coast also grow clams. The main types of clams available from these growers are Manila and Savoury or Varnish clams.

Geoduck (pronounced gooey-duck) clams are being studied for farming on the West Coast. For now, most geoducks are harvested by the Underwater Harvesters Association. These big clams can live up to a metre deep in the ocean floor, and divers direct powerful streams of water around each clam to liquefy the sand so the clam can be easily removed from its hiding place. Geoducks are a prized commodity in Asia and top dollar is paid for high-quality specimens. Here, we're not so fussy about something that looks hard to pronounce and is usually unknown to most consumers. But once you've seen a geoduck, you'll never forget it. The shell can be large, as big as your foot, and the clam inside is so big that the shell can't even close all the way around it. The geoduck's most extraordinary feature, however, is its siphon. It is so big that it can never retract into the shell. It is why the geoduck is sometimes nicknamed elephant clam, as the siphon resembles an elephant's trunk. It can also be called a horse clam, since the siphon also resembles a horse's . . . well, you get the idea. When the siphon is lightly poached and thinly sliced, it is a delicious, mild-tasting disc with two round holes in it, making for beautiful presentation. The body of the clam can be sliced or chopped up to add to chowders. If you get a chance to try it, you should.

Mussels: I'm sorry, Prince Edward Island and other parts of Maritime Canada that produce mussels, but your product can't hold a candle to BC honey mussels produced on the West Coast, especially those from Dale Williamson at BC Honey Mussels (www.facebook.com/bc.honeymussel) in the Northern Gulf Islands and from Saltspring Island Mussels (www.saltspringislandmussels.com) in Ganges. These producers bring to market large mussels with a distinctive golden hue to shells that are filled with plump meat in a much larger meat-to-shell ratio than most other mussels I've tasted. The flavour is also spectacular—definitely sweet, and with none of the somewhat marshy undertone that can sometimes spoil the entire mussel-eating experience. You may have to do a bit of phoning around to fishmongers to see if they have them in stock, as they can sometimes be hard to come by. I once sent two of my friends to a church parking lot near the Departure Bay ferry terminal so they could meet a BC Honey Mussels grower who was going to be in the area at the time. They felt as though the rendezvous and exchange of goods for money smacked of a drug deal. Luckily, they didn't have to do any explaining to the RCMP! An easier way to obtain BC Honey Mussels products is through Mikuni Wild Harvest (www.mikuniwildharvest.com).

Direct-Buy and Community Supported Fisheries (CSF): Some of your best bets for finding a high-quality supply of West Coast seafood may be on the docks or at your local farmers' market. Visiting a port where fishers

Discarded shells from thousands of shucked oysters create an impressive wall of calcium near the Fanny Bay Oysters processing plant.

bring in their catch is definitely fun, although you'll have to do some work to figure out a fisher's schedule (always subject to change) and what they might have available. Always ask to see the catch before you buy, and ask when it was caught. If a boat has been out for many days, or even a week, you may be better off buying a fish that was frozen soon after it was caught instead of a fresh fish. More and more fishers are also showing up at farmers' markets with frozen or canned product. It's a good opportunity to chat and ask about the sustainable-fishing techniques now practised by many smaller fishers. You could also look into getting a year-round supply of seafood through a community-supported fishery. These are like community-supported agriculture programs, but instead of paying a farmer upfront for a share in the upcoming crops, you pay a fisher upfront for a share of whatever they catch in the coming season. Fishing has become a lot more expensive on the West Coast due to higher fuel costs, the general cost of running a boat, and lower wholesale prices. The money you pay in advance can really help out what is usually a family-run operation. At this time, there aren't many CSFs operating in our region, but I'm sure there will be more in the near future. In the meantime, you might want to try Michelle Rose CSF (www.michellerosecsf.com) out of Cowichan Bay. Also, look over the list of vendors that most farmers' markets post on their websites to see if they feature any seafood vendors.

GET FRESH !

🍎

FRESH
&
LOCAL

WELCOME TO
FAIRFIELD MARKET

Fairfield Market marks a welcome return to corner grocery stores that specialize in locally grown produce.

SPECIALTY SHOPS

I am drawn to specialty food shops in our region like a fly to honey. The great thing is that more shop owners are putting their faith in local food and beverage producers to help stock their shelves, and giving them a chance to get known. When an artisan decides to sell to a retailer, it is a major decision that usually requires a greater capital expense, perhaps a profit-sharing arrangement with a distributor, and a much more important commitment to providing what they make on a regular basis—sometimes on a moment's notice. I am very thankful that there are a growing number of shops here that make it easier for island artisans to promote and sell their products. On the other hand, I admit that I am not an ideological everything-I-eat-must-be-local kind of guy. I enjoy eating foods that we can't produce here or are a specialty of a different country. My happiest places are shops that carry some of each, as you'll see in the list below.

COMMUNITY FARM STORE—DUNCAN, AND EDIBLE ISLAND WHOLE FOODS MARKET—COURTENAY

Because I live so close to Duncan, the Community Farm Store has become my go-to place for all the good things I can't find anywhere else. I'm talking a wide range of certified organic products, from emmer (an ancient grain) to local products like hazelnut oil, with a bonus of fresh, local organic produce in season. The dried-foods section has no rival in the area, except when I am up-island, when I stop in at Edible Island Whole Foods Market in Courtenay.

THE MARKET ON YATES—VICTORIA, AND
THE MARKET ON MILLSTREAM—LANGFORD

Many, many years ago, when I was involved with the making of an artisan food product myself, it was time to start selling to retailers and the advice was, "Call Ernie Skinner. He'll probably carry it." And the advice was good. Ernie Skinner, co-founder of the Thrifty Foods chain, is definitely a supporter of local artisans trying to get the word out on their goods. Ernie actually "retired" from Thrifty Foods in 1991, but by 1999 he was back in business with the Market on Yates, and in 2006 he opened the Market on Millstream with his daughter and son-in-law. These are supermarkets with a difference; special attention is paid to particular departments in the store, like fresh meats, seafood, and poultry, and there is an especially nice range of organic produce. Go for a wander and you'll always find something you haven't seen anywhere else.

MCLEAN'S SPECIALTY FOODS—NANAIMO

Eric and Sandy McLean have been presiding over the counter at McLean's for over twenty years now, but they still bring a youthful enthusiasm to their business and the products they sell. They are known primarily for their cheese counter, stocking over a hundred different types of cheese from all over the world. I was also impressed on one visit when Eric offered me a taste of an American-made prosciutto that had been getting raves in culinary circles. Who knew that you would be able to find something

YOU MIGHT ALSO WANT TO TRY:

Shops that are trying to emulate the Market on Yates model with a dedication to local products include:

RED BARN MARKET—FOUR LOCATIONS
ON SOUTH VANCOUVER ISLAND

This small chain was formed in 2009 by four former Thrifty Foods managers, and there are more in the works. You'll find lots of local berries and vegetables in season, decent gluten-free sections, and large deli counters complete with house-made sausages and burgers.

Victoria's Niagara Grocery was founded in 1906. Once reduced to selling cigarettes and porno magazines, it's now a hub for neighbours to find local produce.

like that in a shop in Nanaimo, British Columbia? Due to Eric's Scottish heritage, you will also find a long list of goods from the British Isles and from elsewhere in the Commonwealth, like South Africa.

NIAGARA GROCERY—VICTORIA, AND FAIRFIELD MARKET—VICTORIA

Farmers' markets have become a go-to place to find local foods these days, but there are other options, especially in Victoria with the Niagara Grocery in James Bay and the Fairfield Market in Fairfield. They may be fairly new corner grocery stores, but the buildings themselves are full of history. The Niagara Grocery was discovered by Ken Winchester and Jennifer McKimmie, refugees from the corporate world looking for something different to do. The Niagara Grocery is Victoria's oldest grocery store. It was founded in 1906, but had fallen on rough times with the change in our shopping habits. Ken told me this long-time grocery had gone downhill and morphed into the "corner smokes" store. "There used to be over two hundred corner grocery stores in Victoria and now there are maybe six or eight. Then these neighbourhoods started to come back with more interest in local foods, so that's why we're trying to save two of these old stores." When you approach these stores you definitely get that old-time grocery feel from them; they are not all shiny and metal and antiseptic. They fit in with their neighbourhoods. They're notable for what they don't have—no cigarettes, videos, or porn magazines—but also very notable for what they do have—local and organic produce whenever possible, starting with honey extracted from beehives just down the street and spreading out from there to a range of locally produced foods. Ken and Jennifer have since sold the Fairfield Market to new owners, who are so far carrying on the tradition of stocking local foods.

Old Country Market—Coombs

I hadn't been to the Old Country Market (better known as Goats on the Roof) in Coombs for years. It used to be a favourite stop on my way to Port Alberni and on to the wonderful beaches at Tofino. I didn't think it was worth visiting anymore because it seemed to have become more of a tourist trap, with kitschy shops sprawling around it, instead of the friendly little market with the goats that lived on the roof. "Goats? On the roof?" my wife asked during a drive down-island. I knew it was pointless to argue and we made the quick detour off the highway. Goats still gambol on the roof, the kitschy shops are still there, but when we walked into the actual Old Country Market, I was blown away. The market has been expanded, with a separate kiosk up the lane for fresh, local produce, in case lots if you want. There are huge departments crammed with local and imported food ingredients, glassware, tableware, and wrought iron. There are long counters stocked with dozens of different kinds of cheeses, meats, pastries, and breads, and a double-length ice-cream counter to cut down on lineups in the busy summer hours. You may think of grabbing a little plastic shopping basket to carry around, but save yourself some time and start with a full-sized shopping cart.

Ottavio Italian Bakery and Delicatessen—Oak Bay

Ottavio's is one of those shops that makes life so easy and so difficult. It's easy because you can go there for local and imported cheeses, deli meats, breads, pastries, a wide range of high-quality processed foods, coffee, breakfast, or lunch. It's difficult because the selection is so good, you have a hard time choosing what you want. I have a problem from the moment I step in the door. Do I go and check out the cheeses first? Or the olive oils and vinegars? The cookies? The house-made gelato? The grilled panini? This is a shop that requires repeated visits. It's also a third-generation, family-run business that has ties to the Italian Bakery on Quadra Street in Victoria, and current owners Andrew Moyer and Monica Pozzolo keep their family in mind; they try to make sure at least one of them is there during all business hours, but they also take family days: Ottavio's is closed on Sundays and Mondays.

THE ROOT CELLAR VILLAGE GREEN GROCER—SAANICH AND VICTORIA

I had often driven by the Root Cellar without dropping in until a friend told me it was the best place to find the large quantities of produce I needed for my various canning projects. They were right. From the first time I went in, I was hooked. Adam and Daisy Orser and Phil Lafreniere have put together a huge variety of fresh produce in their ever-expanding shop on McKenzie Avenue. There is an emphasis on local, especially during the growing season, then BC, and then beyond, when they need to provide products that people want, especially in the organic range. The original store underwent a huge expansion in 2013 when they took over a plant nursery next door and, among other improvements, installed a full-service butcher shop (called the Chop Shop) stocked with local meats. "I brought in three real butchers to run the counter," Adam told me. "These are guys who have worked right from the abattoir level to the retail trade, so they know what they're doing." With demands for a shop closer to downtown

> ### FOR ITALIAN, YOU MIGHT ALSO WANT TO TRY:
> #### CHARELLI'S—VICTORIA
> Kind of like Ottavio's but with a lot crammed into a small space.
> #### ITALIAN FOOD IMPORTS—VICTORIA
> This long-time Victoria institution usually has a lineup out the front door at lunchtime of people waiting for made-to-order deli sandwiches. Try the meatball sandwich. There is also a lot of Italian products like pastas and pestos, meats, and cheeses. Very friendly and helpful service.

Victoria, a smaller version of the Root Cellar is slated to open in the spring of 2014 at Hillside and Prior on the site of an old corner store.

VICTORIA PUBLIC MARKET AT THE HUDSON—VICTORIA

The Victoria Public Market is a dream come true for local food lovers. For years, the Downtown Public Market Society fundraised, lobbied, and cajoled their way toward creating an indoor-outdoor public market with the emphasis on local products. The dream came true in the fall of 2013 as the market moved into the ground floor of the iconic Hudson building, former home to the Bay, Canada's oldest department store chain. It's a real coup to get this space, and the message is: People want local food, and if you try hard enough, you can make it available 365 days a year in the heart of a downtown metropolis that had been in danger of becoming a food desert. Market General Manager Maryanne Carmack and a very dedicated Market Society Board have put together an amazing array of vendors in the main market space to try to cover all your food needs. There's a fish shop, a cheese shop, a butcher, a greengrocer, a bakery, a spice shop featuring locally made sea salt, and much more. Local farmers and producers can rent tables inside on a daily basis or join in weekly for a year-long outdoor street market on Wednesdays. There's also a commercial kitchen, used for cooking demos and classes, which can be rented for small processors to create their products in a well-equipped, food-safe environment. Ironically, this new market is right beside where the old Victoria Public Market used to exist, but it was demolished in 1960.

WEINBERG'S GOOD FOOD—FANNY BAY

This is a shop you barely expect to exist, tucked away under the back end of the gas station and sandwich shop at the Buckley Bay ferry terminal and next to the Fanny Bay seafood shop. But from the moment you go inside, you realize that it's not a convenience store designed to gouge ferry passengers waiting for the next trip to Denman and Hornby Islands; it's actually a real grocery store that carries artisan products and baked goods from the immediate area as well as frozen meats like beef and lamb from local ranchers. As the salutation on its website says, "Sometimes missing the boat ain't so bad."

Get fresh seafood at Fanny Bay Oysters at the Buckley Bay ferry terminal while waiting to cross to Denman and Quadra Islands.

SUGGESTED SATURDAY SOJOURNS

COWICHAN VALLEY

My day in the Cowichan Valley always starts with cappuccino and an orange-coconut brioche at Drumroaster Coffee in Cobble Hill. It's just off the Trans-Canada Highway at Cowichan Bay Road, leaving you with a conundrum: carry on to Duncan, or amble down the hill to Cowichan Bay? Because it's market day, head straight to Duncan and the farmers' market centred on City Square. It's open year-round, and even in the winter you'll find fresh baking, artisan food products, and plenty of conversation with the vendors. If you've frittered away your time and feel peckish, stop in at the Craig Street Brew Pub just down the street from the market. This is a beautifully renovated building constructed in the 1940s. In summer, make your way up to the rooftop patio; on chilly days, sit by the wood-burning fire on the main floor. Try a sampler of the beers produced on-site and choose from a diverse menu of pizzas, burgers, and seafood.

From Duncan make your way to Cowichan Bay, taking the back road from downtown Duncan. Trunk Road turns into Tzouhalem and before you know it, you're at Providence Farm. As you turn into the long driveway you'll see the main building with its gleaming metal roof. Park there and make your way into the back area, where you can see fruit trees, the community gardens tended by seniors, the plant nursery with anything you need for your garden, and the farm shop featuring foods produced on the farm.

Follow the curves to Cowichan Bay, where you will want to stop in at Cowichan Bay Seafood for a live crab or fresh fish to take home. Don't worry; they will gladly pack it in ice for you. Pick up a baguette or other baked goods at True Grain Bread and you're probably well into mid-afternoon. If you need to chill out, head to Merridale Cidery on the other side of the highway for a casual cider tasting and then, for a gourmet dinner, down the road from Merridale is Amusé, a charming restaurant in a restored farmhouse overlooking the Unsworth Vineyards. Chef Bradley Boisvert uses as many local ingredients as possible and has a real flair for modern West Coast cuisine.

COMOX VALLEY

You may notice a trend in my suggested day trips. They all include visits to a farmers' or public market. But this is where a lot of the food culture in a community originates, and the Comox Valley Farmers' Market is no exception. The important news is that if you get an early start, you can have breakfast at the market; sometimes it's chef Kathy Jerritt's delicious crepes from Tria Fine Catering and Gourmet Eats, or maybe you'd like to try one or two different tamales from the Hot Tamales Mexican Foods stand. The best thing about this market is that it really is a *farmers'* market. I see a diversity and abundance of produce here that not all markets can match, and it's the only place where I've managed to find some *padron* pepper plants for my garden. After the market I recommend a visit (in season) to Natures Way Farm for fresh organic blueberries and strawberries. You can also taste your way through George Ehrler's excellent line of fruit wine from his Blue Moon Winery. If you're nice, I'm sure he'll show you where all the winemaking takes place, just behind the wine shop and teaching kitchen.

From Courtenay, make your way over to Comox along the water. You can stop at Portuguese Joe's for fresh seafood if you plan to cook at home later. If you're hungry, I have two options, one very casual, the other just a little upscale. First, casual. Sushi Kobo is tucked away on Comox Avenue, and if you blink you'll miss it. Sushi Kobo is primarily a takeout restaurant, but there is a counter with seats inside and a few tables out on the sidewalk. This is my dream come true: an experienced Japanese sushi master comes to Canada and decides to set up shop in a small BC town. The sushi here is made to order. You might have to wait awhile as the shop can get busy, but the wait is worth it. And the staff here cares about their product: a sign at the counter says, "Sushi MUST be eaten fresh! We do not recommend you keep sushi after 4 hours; even in the fridge. Sushi will cry . . ." If you want something a little more upscale, head back Portuguese Joe's way and right beside the Shell gas station you'll find Avenue Bistro. I've never had a bad meal here. Excellent food and stellar service, with local ingredients and BC wines. If you have some time to kill after lunch, I suggest heading back into Courtenay and wending your way down the couple of main streets, stopping in at Edible Island for a look at their very decent array of fresh natural foods and massive dried-foods section, and there are always gelato and snacks to be had at Hot Chocolates on 5th Avenue. Secret place for best coffee? The bicycle shop, of course.

The Broken Spoke on Fitzgerald Avenue will fix your bike or sell you a new one, or you can just sit down in the comfy café side and enjoy a caffeinated beverage featuring Discovery Coffee of Victoria. To work up your appetite for dinner, park your car at Locals Restaurant and walk the pathway along the Courtenay River. As sun sets, ask for a window or patio seat at Locals and enjoy a meal made with all the local ingredients you've been sampling throughout the day. Chef Ronald St. Pierre will be at the stoves, but his wife, Tricia, runs the front of house and will be more than pleased to answer any questions you have about the sources of ingredients. Chances are, you met some of the producers at the market in the morning!

SALT SPRING ISLAND

I know that ferry rides are expensive. If BC Ferries had a "frequent sailor" card, I'm sure I would make it into the top tier. But don't let a short ferry ride put you off from a day trip to Salt Spring Island. Get together with a group of friends and share the cost of the ferry, but make sure you leave room in the trunk for your cameras, a cooler, and the bags of goodies you're sure to be packing on your return. The Saturday Market in Ganges is a delightful mix of arts and crafts and lots and lots of farmers and food producers. Make a point of finding the booth for Salt Spring Sprouts and Mushrooms. Buy a bag of sprouted peanuts and get ready to be addicted to their crunchy, fresh flavour. Taste some of the creative jammy concoctions from Melanie Mulherin at SaltSpring Kitchen Company and if you're lucky, Andrea LeBorgne at Monsoon Coast will have a Thermos full of hot chai for you to sample, made from her Railway Chai spice mix. Grab a baguette from your favourite baker on-site—you'll need it later— and maybe some pastries from Bite Me! Treats or French delights from Brigitte, either at the market or at her bakery, Rendezvous, at Harbour's End at the Ganges Marina.

On the waterfront, not far from the market, you will likely find live crab for sale, and maybe some salmon or prawns depending on the time of year. (This is where the cooler comes in for the first time.) Don't have a pot big enough cook the crab? Drop by the Housewares Store in Mouat's Trading in Ganges, where all your kitchen gear needs will be met. If you want to see how fruits and vegetables are grown, just outside Ganges stop in at the Harbour House Hotel, where the organic garden and farm is always open to the public. Depending on the time of year, you'll get to see some lambs frolicking in the meadow—very good photo opportunities! You may have sampled some of David Wood's Salt Spring Island Cheese at the market, but save room for more sampling of a wider variety of his products and other tasty edibles at his farm on Reynolds Road: cheese, crackers, olives, tapenades, everything you need for a great picnic spread. Now that baguette comes into play as you head to Ruckle Provincial Park. Carry on past the campground to the day-use area and you'll find picnic tables with a fine view of boats and ferries passing by as you dine on your chosen delectables.

If you are totally into knives for your kitchen, you should make an appointment to check out Seth Burton's Cosmo Knives. He is probably the only knife maker of top calibre in western Canada, and he takes custom orders. By now you might want to head back to the ferry to Swartz Bay.

Leave yourself enough time to have dinner at Matt Rissling's Rock Salt Restaurant and Café, right beside the Fulford Harbour ferry terminal. Saturdays are Mexican nights, courtesy of the Rock Salt's sous-chef, Joel Trejo, who grew up in Mexico and spent five years at a culinary university in Mexico City. As you see the ferry coming in, head back to your car, check the ice in your cooler, and reflect on a day well spent; now you're finishing it with a mini ocean cruise back to Swartz Bay.

VICTORIA

So many options, so little time. This is just one way I would spend my day in the city. Because I am of Italian heritage, I would start at Ottavio in Oak Bay. A cappuccino, a pastry, and the Style section of the *Globe and Mail* get me going. (My wife gets the Arts section containing the cryptic puzzle.) Food columnist Lucy Waverman or a guest chef may have a recipe that inspires me for a Sunday dinner, but ingredient gathering starts today. If the recipe has any Italian or European overtones, it's likely I can find what I need right there at Ottavio in the way of cheeses, pastas, and any special flavourings like capers or anchovy paste. From Ottavio, a quick wander down the street into the building that houses both the Whole Beast Salumeria and the Village Butcher. At the Whole Beast, Cory Pelan might tempt me with some truffled sausage or perhaps a Chinese-style pork belly, while the folks behind the counter at the Village Butcher will offer up a locally raised chicken or perhaps cut a piece of brisket just the way I like it for brining and smoking at home. By then it's lunchtime and I might have an urge for noodles or dim sum. If the "yen" is for noodles, then it's J&J Wonton Noodle House on Fort Street, where the noodles and wontons are made in-house. If it's dim sum, then it's over to Don Mee on Fisgard Street, where this restaurant has been at the heart of the Chinatown scene in Victoria for over eighty years. They still push around the dim-sum carts at lunchtime, the servers lifting the lids to tempt you with whatever little gems are inside. I love the sticky rice with chunks of sweet Chinese sausage and the *har gow*, delicate steamed shrimp dumplings.

After rolling out from either of those restaurants, I would stretch my legs to my two favourite places to find cookbooks: Russell Books on Fort Street and Munro's Books on Government Street. Russell has a wide selection of used and out-of-print cookbooks and books on general gastronomy; Munro's is where I find all the latest and greatest in food, including some of my favourite food magazines like *Saveur* and *Jamie*. I usually leave with a heavy tote bag full of books.

For a rest, it's down to the foot of Fort Street and a gin fizz at Little Jumbo, a cocktail bar and restaurant owned and operated by master mixologist Shawn Soole. Gin fizzes are cold, tart, and sweet at the same time, a good pick-me-up for the eating ahead at Zambri's, which has long been my favourite Italian restaurant anywhere in BC. Known for his use of seasonal, local ingredients, chef Peter Zambri never disappoints.

This is just one of the ways I would spend my day in Victoria when food is the main focus.

Saanich Peninsula

This is another region of Vancouver Island that you can't really do justice to in one day, so you might want to plan an overnight stay. Or if you're based in Victoria, make sure you get out there on a regular basis on the weekends, especially at the height of the harvest season. Skip breakfast at home and make an early beeline for the Roost Farm Centre, not far from the Victoria airport. Head into the bakery for a hearty breakfast with breads made from wheat grown and milled on the property. Many of the other ingredients in their omelettes or Bennies come from the farm as well. If you're not in a hurry, you can visit the on-site winery. But if you are looking for more ingredients for a dinner, the North Saanich Farm Market should be your next stop. If the market is closed for the season, you can still check the website for vendors who have farm-gate shops or pop-up market sales in the off-season. I highly recommend making an appointment to visit and taste at Fruit Trees and More in North Saanich. Bob and Verna Duncan have amassed a vast collection of fruit trees—over three hundred varieties at last count—on a relatively small piece of land. Late summer is the best time to visit, when many of the trees are fruiting, but in mid-winter you could also expect to see lemons, limes, oranges, pomelos, and other warm-climate fruits hanging from branches, either outside in the balmy clime of the peninsula or inside a densely leafy, unheated greenhouse. Bob propagates trees for sale. I have an olive tree and two varieties of plum doing well in my backyard right now, thanks to Bob's wizardry. Ask Verna if she has any samples of her luscious lemon bars and marmalades made from citrus fruit grown on their property.

As you make your way back down the peninsula, check out Muffett & Louisa on Beacon Avenue in Sidney for the latest in kitchenware and linens, and if you're dining at home, browse the fresh seafood available at the Satellite Fish Market on the water right at the end of Beacon Avenue. For a late lunch and tasting session, the Sea Cider ciderhouse is tucked behind an apple orchard not far from the Mount Newton Cross Road turnoff from the Pat Bay Highway. Taste the full range of ciders in short or long flights as you nibble on their Artisan Lunch Plate, which features BC-made meats and cheeses such as the Bleu Clair from Little Qualicum Cheeseworks. When you're full of food, walk it off amidst the splendid foliage of the Butchart Gardens, where you can get enough exercise to work up your appetite once again for afternoon tea. Reservations recommended.

SUGGESTED READING

I'm all about sustainable production, local and organic when possible, and smart shopping.

Here are some of the books I've read over the years that have helped me develop my philosophy of using the money I budget for food.

The 100-Mile Diet: A Year of Local Eating, Alisa Smith and J.B. MacKinnon (Vintage Canada, 2007). This is the book that has been the inspiration for many locally sourced diets, and it remains a sometimes whimsical look into the tough chore that faced Vancouver apartment dwellers Smith and MacKinnon: they started their diet in the springtime when there was barely a leaf of local lettuce to be found near their home.

The Omnivore's Dilemma: A Natural History of Four Meals, Michael Pollan (The Penguin Press, 2006). Pollan, a professor of journalism and author of three previous books, really hit the mark with this tome that asks all the right questions about where our food comes from and how we should eat. His follow-up to *The Omnivore's Dilemma*, *In Defense of Food: An Eater's Manifesto*, in 2008, offered this motto: "Eat food. Not too much. Mostly plants."

Bottomfeeder: How to Eat Ethically in a World of Vanishing Seafood, Taras Grescoe (Bloomsbury USA, 2008). Montreal-based freelance writer Grescoe travelled the world to bring us the ethical lowdown on the world of seafood. He investigates many of the major species we need to be concerned about: salmon, tuna, and shrimp.

The Urban Food Revolution: Changing the Way We Feed Cities, Peter Ladner (New Society Publishers, 2011). Peter Ladner is a former Vancouver city councillor and co-founder of the *Business in Vancouver* weekly newspaper, so he sees food in the city from a journalistic and political side. This well-researched book looks at some common myths about our food system and how we can get more local food back into our urban lifestyles.

All the Dirt: Reflections on Organic Farming, Rachel Fisher, Heather Stretch, Robin Tunnicliffe (TouchWood Editions, 2012). If you have ever wondered how farmers do it, or have considered getting into farming yourself, even on a small scale, this is the book for you. These farmers have done it all, through bad weather, pests, and Monsanto. Honest and forthright, it amazes you that they have been able to triumph in careers that are almost set up to fail from the start.

Island Wineries of British Columbia, Gary Hynes, updated and expanded (TouchWood Editions, 2013). This book covers the ever-changing world of wine in this region. With fascinating profiles of all the winery owners and recipes featuring their products.

On the Flavour Trail, Island Chefs' Collaborative, edited by Christabel Padmore (TouchWood Editions, 2013). With all of the great food being produced on Vancouver Island and the Gulf Islands, you need something handy to help you cook with it. This is it, with recipes from some of the region's top chefs.

1 Blue Moon Estate Winery
4905 Darcy Road, Courtenay V9J 1R5
(250) 338-9765
www.bluemoonwinery.ca,
George Ehrler

2 Dark Side Chocolates
Suite 1-2722 Dunsmuir Avenue,
Cumberland V0R 1S0
(250) 336-0126
www.darksidechocolates.com,
Allison Mackenzie

3 Denman Bakery
556 5th Street, Courtenay V9N 1K3
(250) 871-0880
Bill Marler

4 Edible Island Whole Foods Market
477 6th Street, Courtenay V9N 6V4
(250) 334-3116
www.edibleisland.ca,

5 Estevan Tuna
4098 Gartley Point Road,
Courtenay V9N 9T2
(250) 334-2929
www.bctuna.com,
Bruce Devereux

6 Fanny Bay Oysters
P.O. Box 209, Union Bay V0R 3B0
(877) 335-0125 or (250) 335-0125
www.fannybayoysters.com

7 Gunter Brothers Meats
6200 Ledingham Road,
Courtenay V9J 1M5
(250) 334-2960

Dennis and Harry Gunter

8 Hot Chocolates
368 5th Street, Courtenay V9N 2M7
(250) 338-8211
hotchocolates.ca,

9 LegatoGelato
529 Holiday Road,
Fanny Bay V0R 1W0
(250) 335-1676
www.legatogelato.ca,
Jaki Ayton and Karen Fouracre

10 Locals Restaurant
1760 Riverside Lane,
Courtenay V9N 8C7
250-338-6493
www.localscomoxvalley.com,
Chef Ronald St. Pierre
and Tricia St. Pierre

11 Natural Pastures Cheese Company
635 McPhee Avenue,
Courtenay V9N 2Z7
(250) 334-4422
www.naturalpastures.com,
Phillip, Edgar, and Doug Smith

12 Portuguese Joe's Fish Market
3025 Comox Road,
Courtenay V9N 3P7
(250) 339-2119

13 Prontissima Pasta
Suite C-2384 Rosewall Crescent,
Courtenay V9N 8R9
(250) 338-3636
www.prontissimapasta.com,
Sarah and Derek Walsh

14 Royston Roasting Company
3904 Island Highway South,
Royston V0R 2V0
(250) 871-8666
bccoffee.ca,
Gary and Dyan Spink

15 Shelter Point Distillery
4650 Regent Road,
Campbell River V9H 1E3
(778) 420-2200
shelterpointdistillery.com,
Patrick Evans and James Marinus

16 Tannadice Farms
3465 Burns Road,
Courtenay V9J 1S3
(250) 338-8239
www.tannadicefarms.com
Heather and Allen McWilliam

17 Tria Fine Catering and Gourmet Eats
1279 5th Street,
Courtenay V9N 1L7
(250) 871-8716
www.triaculinarystudio.ca,
Chef Kathy Jerritt

18 Weinberg's Good Food
6856 South Island Highway,
Fanny Bay V0R 1W0
www.weinbergsfood.com,
(250) 335-1534
Leah Weinberg

COMOX
VALLEY

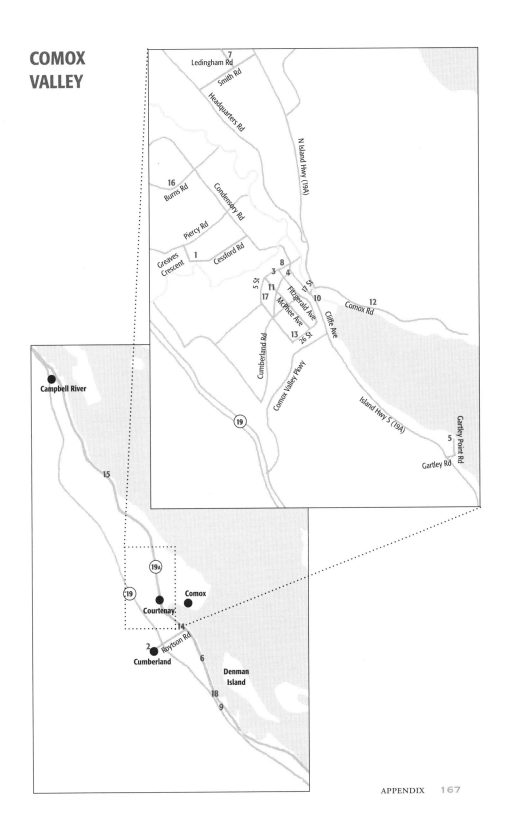

Ledingham Rd
Smith Rd
Headquarters Rd
N Island Hwy (19A)
Burns Rd
Condensory Rd
Piercy Rd
Cessford Rd
Greaves Crescent
5 St
17 St
Fitzgerald Ave
McPhee Ave
Cumberland Rd
26 St
Cliffe Ave
Comox Rd
Comox Valley Pkwy
Island Hwy S (19A)
Gartley Point Rd
Gartley Rd

Campbell River
Courtenay
Comox
Cumberland
Royston Rd
Denman Island

1 **Alderlea Farm and Café**
3390 Glenora Road, Glenora V9L 6S1
(250) 715-0799
www.alderleafarm.com, ⨏
John and Katy Ehrlich

2 **Bigleaf Maple Syrup Festival**
To reach syrup producers, contact
the BC Forest Discovery Centre
2892 Drinkwater Road,
Duncan V9L 6C2
(250) 715-1113
www.blmaple.net

3 **Cheese Pointe Farm**
1282 Cherry Point Road,
Cowichan Bay V0R 1N2
(250) 715-8565
⨏
Hilary and Patty Abbott

4 **Cherry Point Estate Wines**
840 Cherry Point Road,
Cowichan Bay V0R 1L3
(250) 743-1272
cherrypointestatewines.com, ⨏
Xavier and Maria-Clara Bonilla

5 **Community Farm Store**
Suite 101-330 Duncan Street,
Duncan V9L 3W4
(250) 748-6227
www.communityfarmstore.ca, ⨏

6 **Cowichan Bay Seafood**
1751 Cowichan Bay Road,
Cowichan Bay V0R 1N0
(250) 748-0020
www.cowichanbayseafood.com, ⨏
Anne and Gregg Best

7 **Cowichan Valley Meat Market**
5191 Koksilah Frontage Road,
Duncan V9L 6V6
(250) 746-8732

8 **Deerholme Farm**
4830 Stelfox Road, Duncan V9L 6S9
(250) 748-7450
www.deerholme.com, ⨏
Chef Bill Jones

9 **Drumroaster Coffee**
24-1400 Cowichan Bay Road,
Cobble Hill V0R 1L3
(250) 743-5200
www.drumroaster.com, ⨏
Geir and Carsen Oglend

10 **Fairburn Water Buffalo**
3330 Jackson Road, Duncan V9L 6N7
250-746-4621
www.fairburnwaterbuffalo.com, ⨏
The Archer family: Darrel, Anthea,
Maryann, and Richard

11 **Island Farmhouse Poultry**
1615 Koksilah Road,
Cowichan Bay V0R 1N1
(250) 746-6163
www.farmhousepoultry.ca
Lyle Young

12 **Kilrenny Farm**
1470 Cowichan Bay Road,
Cowichan Bay V0R 1N1
(250) 743-9019
www.kilrennyfarm.com
Russ and Deborah Fahlman

13 **Mad Dog Crabs**
775 Canada Avenue,
Duncan V9L 1V1
www.maddogcrabs.ca, ⨏
(250) 715-0206
Scott and Katie Mahon

14 **Merridale Estate Cidery**
1230 Merridale Road,
Cobble Hill V0R 1L0
(250) 743-4293
www.merridalecider.com, ⨏
Janet Docherty and Rick Pipes

15 **Moziro Coffee**
1761 Shawnigan-Mill Bay Road,
Shawnigan Lake V0R 2W0
(250) 510-6720
www.moziro.com, ⨏

16 **Pedrosa's Asparagus Farm**
1550 Robson Lane,
Cowichan Bay V0R 1N1
(250) 733-0700
asparagusfarmplus.com
Jaco Pedrosa

17 **Pots & Paraphernalia**
863 Canada Avenue,
Duncan V9L 1V2
(250) 748-4614
www.potsandparaphernalia.ca, ⨏
Terry Raven

18 **Providence Farm**
1843 Tzouhalem Road,
Duncan V9L 5L6
(250) 746-4204
providence.bc.ca, ⨏

19 **Saison Market Vineyard**
7575 Mays Road,
North Cowichan V9L 6A8
(250) 597-0484
www.saisonmarket.ca
Ingrid Lehwald and Frédéric
Desbiens

20 **Teafarm**
8350 Richards Trail,
North Cowichan V9L 6B4
(250) 748-3811
www.teafarm.ca, ⨏
Victor Vesely and Margit
Nellemann

21 **True Grain Bread**
1725 Cowichan Bay Road,
Cowichan Bay V0R 1N0
(250) 746-7664
www.truegrain.ca, ⨏
Bruce and Leslie Stewart

22 **Venturi-Schulze Vineyards**
4235 Vineyard Road,
Cobble Hill V0R 1L5
(250) 743-5630
www.venturischulze.com, ⨏
Marilyn, Giordano and Michelle

23 **Well-Bred**
9255 Chemainus Road,
Chemainus V0R 1K5
(250) 246-2411
WellBredinChemainus@gmail.
com, ⨏
Mark Primmer and Shannon Peck

COWICHAN VALLEY

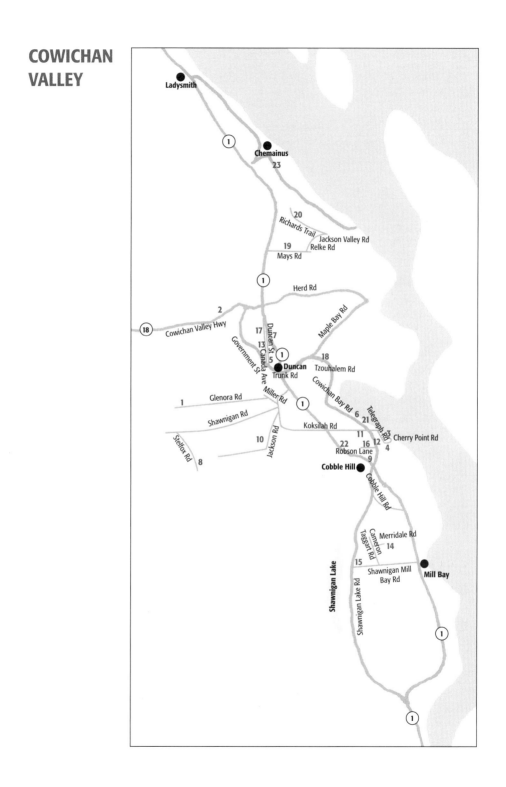

Ladysmith

Chemainus
23

20
Richards Trail
Jackson Valley Rd
19   Relke Rd
Mays Rd

Herd Rd

2
17 Duncan St 7
Cowichan Valley Hwy   13 Canada Ave
18   Government St   5   1   18
Maple Bay Rd
Duncan   Tzouhalem Rd
Trunk Rd
Cowichan Bay Rd
1   Glenora Rd   Miller Rd
Shawnigan Rd   6   21   Telegraph Rd
Stelfox Rd   Koksilah Rd   11   3   Cherry Point Rd
10   22   16   12   4
8   Robson Lane   9

Cobble Hill

Cobble Hill Rd

Cameron Taggart Rd   Merridale Rd
14
15   Shawnigan Mill
Bay Rd   Mill Bay

Shawnigan Lake

Shawnigan Lake Rd

1 **Deacon Vale Farm**
380 Campbell Bay Road,
Mayne Island V0N 2J0
(250) 539-5456
www.deaconvale.com
Don and Shanti McDougall

2 **Denman Island Chocolate**
4321 Denman Road,
Denman Island V0R 1T0
(250) 335-2418
denmanislandchocolate.com, f
Daniel Terry

3 **Harbour House Farm**
121 Upper Ganges Road,
Salt Spring Island V8K 2S2
(250) 537-5571
saltspringharbourhouse.com, f

4 **Island Spirits Distillery**
4605 Roburn Rd,
Hornby Island V0R 1Z0
(250) 335-0630
www.islandspirits.ca
Peter Kimmerly

5 **Love My Kitchen**
140 Fulford-Ganges Road,
Salt Spring Island V8K 2T8
(250) 537-5882
lovemykitchen.ca

6 **Moonstruck Organic Cheese**
1306 Beddis Road,
Salt Spring Island V8K 2C9
(250) 537-4987
www.moonstruckcheese.com, f
Susan and Julia Grace

7 **Mouat's Trading**
106 Fulford-Ganges Road,
Salt Spring Island V8K 2S3
(250) 537-5551 or (877) 490-5593
www.mouatstrading.com

8 **Salish Sea Chocolate Company**
229 Meadow Drive,
Salt Spring Island V8K 1T9
(250) 653-0090
www.salishseachocolate.ca

9 **Salt Spring Bread Company**
251 Forest Ridge Road,
Salt Spring Island V8K
(250) 653-4809
www.phillipvanhorndesign.com/
bakery
Heather Campbell

10 **Salt Spring Coffee**
109 McPhillips Avenue,
Salt Spring Island V8K 2T6
(250) 537-0825
www.saltspringcoffee.com, f

11 **Salt Spring Island Cheese**
285 Reynolds Road,
Salt Spring Island V8K 1Y2
(250) 653-2300
www.saltspringcheese.com, f
David Wood

12 **SeaChange Seafoods**
334 Upper Ganges Road, Unit 100,
Salt Spring Island V8K 1R7
(250) 537-5641 or
(888) 747-5641 ext. 0
seachangeseafoodsandgifts.ca, f
John and Anne Millerd

13 **Soya Nova Tofu Company**
1200 Beddis Road,
Salt Spring Island V8K 2C8
(250) 537-9651
soyanova.com, f
Debbie Lauzon

GULF ISLANDS

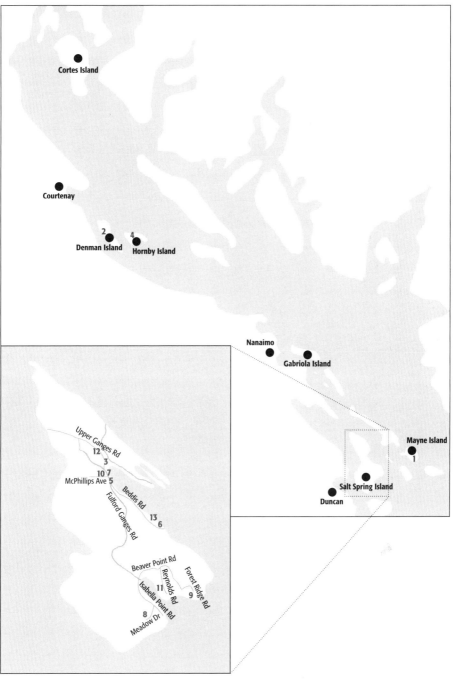

Cortes Island

Courtenay

2 Denman Island

4 Hornby Island

Nanaimo

Gabriola Island

Mayne Island
1

Salt Spring Island

Duncan

Upper Ganges Rd

12

3

10 7

McPhillips Ave 5

Beddis Rd

Fulford Ganges Rd

13 6

Beaver Point Rd

Reynolds Rd

Forest Ridge Rd

11

Isabella Point Rd

9

8

Meadow Dr

NANAIMO AND SURROUNDING AREA

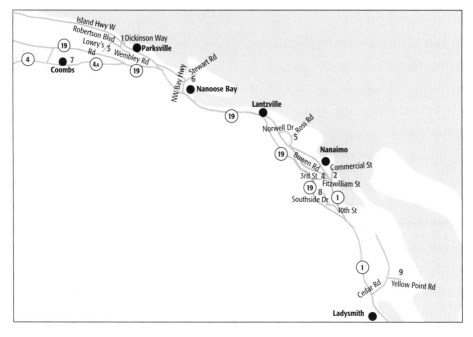

1 Artisan Edibles
895 Dickinson Way,
Parksville, V9P 2H2
(250) 248-0670
artisanedibles.com, [f]
Maureen Drew

2 Flying Fish
180 Commercial Street,
Nanaimo V9R 5G6
(250) 754-2104
www.flyingfishnanaimo.ca, [f]
Glen Saunders

3 Little Qualicum Cheeseworks
403 Lowry's Road,
Parksville V9P 2B5
(250) 954-3931
www.cheeseworks.ca, [f]
Clarke and Nancy Gourlay

4 McLean's Specialty Foods
426 Fitzwilliam Street,
Nanaimo V9R 3B1
(250) 754-0100
mcleansfoods.com, [f]
Eric and Sandy McLean

5 Nanaimo Sausage House
3018 Ross Road,
Nanaimo V9T 3Z1
(250) 751-0555
[f]
Catherine Clarke

6 Nanoose Edibles
1960 Stewart Road,
Nanoose Bay V9P 9E7
(250) 468-2332
[f]
Lorne and Barbara Ebell

7 Old Country Market
2326 Alberni Highway,
Coombs V0R 1M0
(250) 248-6272
www.oldcountrymarket.com, [f]

8 St. Jean's Cannery
242 Southside Drive,
Nanaimo V9R 6Z5
(250) 754-2185
www.stjeans.com, [f]

9 Yellow Point Cranberries
4532 Yellow Point Road,
Ladysmith V9G 1G5
(250) 245-5283
www.yellowpointcranberries.com
Grant Keefer

SAANICH PENINSULA

1 Babe's Honey
4150 Blenkinsop Road,
Victoria V8X 2C4
(250) 658-8319
www.babes-honey-farm.com,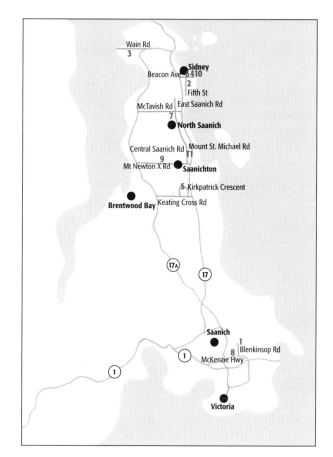
Brandon Schwartz

2 Capital Iron
Sidney Centre
9764 Fifth Street, Sidney, V8L 2X2
(250) 655-7115
www.capitaliron.net,

3 Fruit Trees and More
724 Wain Road,
North Saanich V8L 5N8
(250) 656-4269
www.fruittreesandmore.com
Bob and Verna Duncan

4 Muffett & Louisa
109-2506 Beacon Avenue,
Sidney V8L 1Y2
(250) 656-0011
www.muffetandlouisa.com,

5 Reg Barber Tampers
#7-6824 Kirkpatrick Crescent,
Saanichton V8M 1Z9
(250) 544-1778
www.coffeetamper.com,
Reg Barber

6 Rogers' Chocolates
2423 Beacon Avenue,
Sidney V8L 1X5
(250) 655-0305
www.rogerschocolates.com

7 The Roost Farm Centre
9100 East Saanich Road,
North Saanich V8L 1H5
(250) 655-0075
www.roostfarmcentre.com

8 The Root Cellar
Village Green Grocer
1286 McKenzie Avenue,
Victoria V8P 5P2
(250) 477-9495
www.therootcellar.ca,

9 Saanich Organics
1438 Mt Newton X Road,
Saanichton V8M 1S1
(250) 818-5807
saanichorganics.com,
Robin Tunnicliffe, Rachel Fisher,
and Heather Stretch

10 Satellite Fish Company
2550 Beacon Ave, Sidney V8L 1Y2
(250) 656-2642

11 Sea Cider Farm and Ciderhouse
2487 Mount St. Michael Road,
Saanichton V8M 1T7
(250) 544-4824
www.seacider.ca,
Kristen Jordan
Adam and Daisy Orser

GREATER VICTORIA

2% Jazz
1a 1701 Douglas Street,
Victoria V8T 4M1
(250) 590-8282 and
1b 2631 Douglas Street,
Victoria V8T 4M2
(250) 384-5282
2percentjazz.com, ⬛

2 Capital Iron
1900 Store Street, Victoria V8T 4R4
(250) 385-9703
www.capitaliron.net, ⬛

3 Charelli's
2851 Foul Bay Road,
Victoria V8N 5G5
(250) 598-4794
charellis-cheese-shop-and-
delicatessen.myshopify.com, ⬛

4 Choux Choux Charcuterie
830 Fort Street, Victoria V8W 2H6
(250) 382-7572
chouxchouxcharc.com, ⬛
Luke Young and Paige Symonds

5 Cold Comfort Ice Cream
2-1115 North Park Street,
Victoria V8T 1C7
(778) 433-5215
www.coldcomfort.ca, ⬛
Autumn Maxwell

6 Cook Culture
1317 Blanshard Street,
Victoria V8W 0B5
(250) 590-8161
cookculture.com, ⬛
Jed Grieve

7 Cowichan Bay Seafood
In the Victoria Public Market, 1701
Douglas Street, Victoria V8W 0C1
(778) 433-4385
www.cowichanbayseafood.com, ⬛
Anne and Gregg Best

Discovery Coffee
8a Central: 664 Discovery Street,
Victoria V8T 1G9
(250) 477-2323
8b Oak Bay: 1964 Oak Bay Avenue,
Victoria V8R 1E1
(250) 590-7717
8c James Bay: 281 Menzies Street,
Victoria V8V 2G6
(250) 590-6323
www.discoverycoffee.com, ⬛

9 Fairfield Market
1275 Oscar Street, Victoria V8V 2X6
(250) 590-1772
⬛

10 Finest At Sea
27 Erie Street, Victoria V8V 1P8
(250) 383-7760
www.finestatsea.com, ⬛
Bob Fraumeni

11 Fol Epi
101-398 Harbour Road,
Victoria V9A 0B7
(250) 477-8882
folepi.ca, ⬛
Cliff Leir

12 Fry's Red Wheat Bread
416 Craigflower Road,
Victoria V9A 2V8
(250) 590-5727
travelingbaker.tumblr.com, ⬛
Byron Fry

13 Galloping Goose Sausages
4484 Lindholm Road,
Metchosin V9C 3Y1
(250) 474-5788
gallopinggoosesausage.com, ⬛

14 Island Spice Trade
In the Victoria Public Market, 1701
Douglas Street, Victoria V8W 0C1
(778) 433-2862
www.islandspicetrade.ca, ⬛
Andrew Shepherd

15 Italian Bakery
3197 Quadra Street,
Victoria V8X 1E9
(250) 388-4557
italianbakeryquadra.foodpages.ca, ⬛
Alberto Pozzolo

16 Italian Food Imports
1114 Blanshard Street,
Victoria V8W 2H6
(250) 385-7923
Maurizio and Massimo Segato

17 The Little Cheese Shop
1034 Fort Street, Victoria V8V 3K4
(250) 388-5810
⬛
Lauren Van der Haegen

18 The London Chef
953 Fort Street, Victoria V8V 3K3
(250) 590-1865
thelondonchef.com, ⬛
Chef Dan Hayes

19 The Market on Millstream
125-2401C Millstream Road,
Langford V9B 3R5
(250) 391-1110
www.themarketstores.com, ⬛

20 The Market on Yates
903 Yates Street, Victoria V8V 3M4
(250) 381-6000
www.themarketstores.com, ⬛

**21 McLennan's Island
Meat and Seafood**
307 Cook Street, Victoria V8V 3X5
(250) 382-3331
⬛
Lloyd McLennan

22 Murchie's
1110 Government Street,
Victoria V8W 1Y2
(250) 383-3112
www.murchies.com, ⬛

23 Niagara Grocery
579 Niagara Street,
Victoria V8V 1H8
(250) 383-1223
getfreshwithalocal.com, ⬛
Ken Winchester and Jennifer
McKimmie

24 Olive the Senses
In the Victoria Public Market, 1701
Douglas Street, Victoria V8W 0C1
(250) 882-4210
olivethesenses.com, [f]
Steve and Emily Lycopolus

25 Ottavio Italian Bakery and Delicatessen
2272 Oak Bay Ave,
Victoria V8R 1G7
(250) 592-4080
www.ottaviovictoria.com, [f]
Monica Pozzolo and Andrew Moyer

26 Paboom
1437 Store Street, Victoria V8W 3J6
(250) 380-0020
[f]

27 Phillips Soda Works
2010 Government Street,
Victoria V8T 4P1
(250) 380-1912
phillipssoda.com, [f]

Red Barn Market
28a 5550 West Saanich Road,
Victoria V9E 2G1
(250) 479-8349
28b Mattick's Farm: 129-5325 Cordova
Bay Road, Victoria V8Y 2L3
(250) 658-2998
28c Vanalman: 751 Vanalman Avenue,
Victoria V8Z 3B8
(250) 479-6817
28d Latoria Walk: 611 Brookside Road,
Victoria V9C 0C3
(250) 590-8133
redbarnmarket.ca, [f]

Rogers' Chocolates
29a 913 Government Street,
Victoria V8W 1X5
(250) 881-8771
29b Factory Outlet: 4253 Commerce
Circle, Victoria V8Z 4M2
(250) 727-6851
29c Oak Bay: 2234 Oak Bay Ave,
Victoria V8R 1G5
(250) 598-2911
29d Uptown: Unit 129-3551 Uptown
Boulevard, Victoria V8Z 0B9
(778) 433-2604
www.rogerschocolates.com, [f]

30 The Root Cellar Village Green Grocer
1120 Hillside Avenue,
Victoria V8T 2A7
www.therootcellar.ca, [f]
Adam and Daisy Orser

31 Salt Spring Island Cheese
In the Victoria Public Market, 1701
Douglas Street, Victoria V8W 0C1
www.saltspringcheese.com, [f]
David Wood

Silk Road Tea
32a 1624 Government Street,
Victoria V8W 1Z3
(250) 704-2688
32b In the Victoria Public Market, 1701
Douglas Street, Victoria V8W 0C1
(778) 433-9838
www.silkroadteastore.com, [f]
Daniela Cubelic

33 Spinnakers
308 Catherine Street,
Victoria V9A 3S8
(250) 386-2739 or (877)
838-2739
www.spinnakers.com, [f]

34 Stick in the Mud
6715 Eustace Road,
Sooke V9Z 0H1
(250) 642-5635
stickinthemud.ca, [f]

35 Tugwell Creek Honey Farm and Meadery
8750 West Coast Road,
Sooke V9Z 1H2
(250) 642-1956
tugwellcreekfarm.com, [f]
Bob Liptrot and Dana LeComte

36 The Tuscan Kitchen
653 View Street, Victoria V8W 1J8
(250) 386-8191
www.thetuscankitchen.com, [f]
Gerri and Mauro Schelini

37 Victoria Public Market at the Hudson
1701 Douglas Street,
Victoria V8W 0C1
(778) 433-2787
victoriapublicmarket.com, [f]
Maryanne Carmack: General
Manager

38 Village Butcher
2032 Oak Bay Avenue,
Victoria V8R 1E4
(250) 598-1115
villagebutcher.ca, [f]
Michael Windle and Rebecca
Teskey

39 The Whole Beast Artisan Salumeria
2032 Oak Bay Avenue,
Victoria V8R 1E4
(250) 590-7675
thewholebeast.ca
Cory Pelan

40 Wild Fire Bakery
1517 Quadra Street,
Victoria V8W 2L3
(250) 381-3473
www.wildfirebakery.ca, [f]

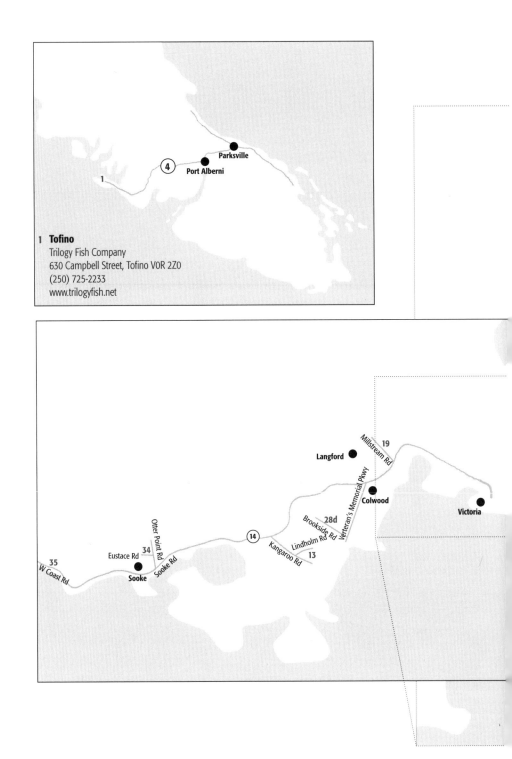

1 Tofino
Trilogy Fish Company
630 Campbell Street, Tofino V0R 2Z0
(250) 725-2233
www.trilogyfish.net

GREATER VICTORIA

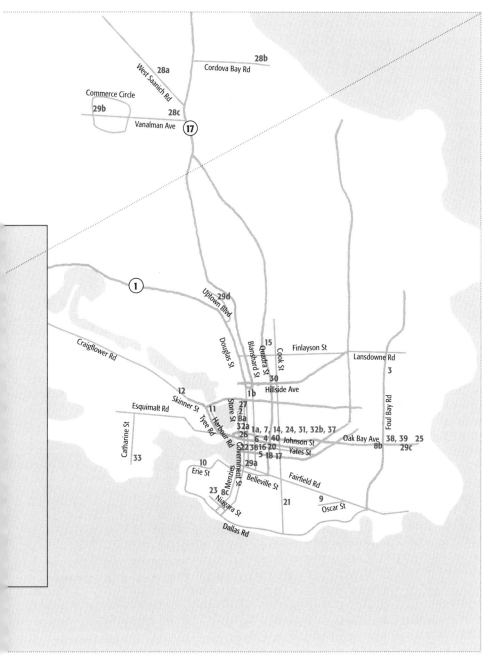

INDEX

ACKNOWLEDGMENTS

My wife, Ramona, is ever at my side as my sounding board and my inspiration. The late, great James Barber was a guiding force from the time I watched him on TV on weekday afternoons as the Urban Peasant. I learned a lot about cooking from him, and when finally I met him, he encouraged me as a food journalist and an ardent lover of the bounty of the Cowichan Valley. In that same way, Chef Bill Jones of Deerholme Farm has been here in the Cowichan to share his techniques, recipes, mushroom finds, and indulge in our mutual zeal for barbecue.

I've also had support from some wonderful people at CBC Radio over the years during various iterations of my food programs. They include program hosts Cecilia Walters, Rick Cluff, Mark Forsythe, and Jo-Ann Roberts, and producers Cathy Simon, Phillip Ditchburn, Karin Konstantynowicz, Anne Penman, Laura Palmer, Laura Green, and Kirstie Hudson. My editor at *Aqua Magazine*, Gail Sjuberg, has been an active advisor on worthy food businesses on Salt Spring Island. And, of course, thanks go to all the food artisans I have met over the years, for their willingness to share the inside story of their struggles and successes with me and my listeners and readers.

DON GENOVA is a Vancouver Island-based award-winning freelance journalist specializing in food and travel. He also teaches cooking classes and courses in food and travel writing and sustainable gastronomy. His stories on radio, television, in print, and on the web share the fascinating backgrounds of farmers and food artisans passionate about what they raise, grow, and produce. His latest radio column with CBC Victoria is called "Food Matters" and delves into the world of sustainable eating in British Columbia.

Don holds a Master of Food Culture from the University of Gastronomic Sciences in Italy in 2007. He also holds a Bachelor of Environmental Science from the University of Waterloo and is an honours graduate of the Humber College Radio Broadcasting Program. Follow Don's blog at http://blog.dongenova.com or on Twitter at @dongenova.